ROBERT BURNS AND HIS RHYMING FRIENDS

AMS PRESS
NEW YORK

ROBERT BURNS

AND HIS

RHYMING FRIENDS

Collected and Edited by

JOHN D. ROSS, LL.D., F.S.A. (Scot.)

Author of "Who's Who in Burns," etc.

With

Bibliographical and Biographical Notes and a Glossary

By

GEORGE F. BLACK, Ph.D.

Author of "Scotland's Mark on America," etc.

ENEAS MACKAY
STIRLING

440629

Library of Congress Cataloging in Publication Data

Ross, John Dawson, 1853-1939, ed.
    Robert Burns and his rhyming friends.

    Reprint of the 1928 ed.
    1. Burns, Robert, 1759-1796, in fiction,
drama, poetry, etc. I. Title.
PR 4335.R68 1974   821'.6   77-144478
ISBN 0-404-08538-5

Reprinted from the edition of 1928, Stirling
First AMS edition published in 1974
Manufactured in the United States of America

AMS PRESS INC.
NEW YORK, N.Y. 10003

CONTENTS

CONTENTS

PREFATORY

THE Preface to *The Burns Rosary*, published in 1923, contains the following :—

"Before Robert Burns died, he had the pleasure of reading a few able tributes to his Genius. Contrary to the opinion held by many people, his ability was not overlooked in his native Scotland, but had even gone farther afield. Editions of his poems appeared during his lifetime in Kilmarnock, Edinburgh, London, Belfast, Philadelphia, and New York. His writings had also been seen frequently in many magazines, journals and newspapers of his time, and his songs in special publications, like Johnson's and Thomson's, while in Broadsides and Chapbooks—more or less authorised—his countrymen had become familiar with his name, and willingly helped to extend his fame. It is true that few scholarly criticisms were made public during the poet's brief earthly career, but for a few years at least he enjoyed the sweets of popular applause, both at home and in a steadily widening circle."

At another time those remarks suggested my assembling in a single group the various rhyming epistles and short poems addressed to the Poet during his lifetime, a compliment that should have been accorded them by some one many years ago. While I possessed many of

these Epistles, there were others that I lacked—
among them a few that had been published
anonymously—and these were somewhat
difficult to obtain, being little known and rarely
met with at this date.   Even friends well versed
in Burns lore whom I consulted regarding them,
advised me that while they were aware such
Poems had appeared in print, yet they had never
seen them, nor could they at the moment assist
me in locating them.   I finally succeeded, however, in securing all I had listed for my purpose,
and doubtless the lovers of Burns will be glad
to possess this collection of those unique and
early appreciations of the Poet's genius, in their
present accessible and pleasing form.

The fragmentary verses addressed to the
Poet by Mrs. Dunlop and other well wishers,
being only of minor importance, have not been
included in the collection, while the mediocre
rhymes of the bombastic *Saunders* Tait have for
other reasons been ignored.

For favours extended to me while engaged in
the compilation of this work I sincerely thank
Mr. Septimus A. Pitt, Librarian of The Mitchell
Library, Glasgow ; Mr. Alexander W. Macphail,
Bookseller and Burns enthusiast, Edinburgh ;
and Miss B. W. Adams of Argyle Crescent,
Portobello, Midlothian.

The extensive biographical and bibliographical data by Dr. George F. Black, attached
to the poems, make it unnecessary for me to
extend this prefatory note to any greater length.

J. D. R.

Inscribed to

*MR. WILLIAM BAXTER, of Tranent,
a man who appreciates the Genius of Robert
Burns and is ever ready to proclaim and expound
the principles of the Universal Brotherhood of
Man, and other predominating features embodied
in the Poet's writings.*

ROBERT BURNS

AND HIS

RHYMING FRIENDS

REPLIES TO BURNS'S "ADDRESS TO THE DEIL."

More than one "Reply" to Burns's "Address to the Deil" was published during the Poet's lifetime, of which the best is certainly that by James Ditchburn, given below. The earliest "Reply" appears to have been the product of Ebenezer Picken, the unfortunate Poet, entitled "The Deil's Answer to his vera Wordy Friend R— B—," which appeared in his "Poems and Epistles, mostly in the Scottish dialect," published in Paisley in 1788. His verses were reprinted in the Appendix to v. 1 of "Sermons by the Rev. John Dun, V.D.M.," published at Kilmarnock by J. Wilson, in 1790. In the Appendix on "The Communion" (v. 1, pp. 257-259), Mr. Dun says: "A late Author indeed, who has abused his God and his King, has ridiculed the Communion in the parish where he lived, under the sarcasm of a Holy Fair. He

11

pretends to be only a ploughman, though he
mixes Latin with his mixture of English and
Scottish, and is not like "Thresher Duck
who kept at flail." He published, *inter alia*, a
profane poetic address to the Devil, which
occasioned what follows—in language similar
to his." Then follow Picken's verses. The
" Deil's Answer " was again reprinted by Picken,
with considerable alterations, in the two volume
edition of his "Miscellaneous Poems," published by subscription in Edinburgh in 1813.
Another "Deil's Reply to Robert Burns," by
David Morrison, appears in the little volume of
" Poems, chiefly in the Scottish Dialect," printed
in Montrose by David Buchanan in 1700, in 12°.
It is in eighteen stanzas in the measure of the
original "Address" as, indeed, are all the
Replies, with a six line introductory rhyme
"To the Reader." An "Answer to the Deil's
Reply to Mr. Burns," by John Learmont appears
in his "Poems, pastoral, satirical, tragic and
comic," published in Edinburgh for the Author
by Alexander Chapman & Co., in 1791. In
1793 appeared "The Deil's Reply to Robert
Burns," dated from Lumley Den, Forfarshire,
September 6th, 1793, and signed "James
Ditchburn, Ushaw Moor." This is by far and
away the best Reply published, and it has been
many times reprinted in pamphlet form and in
newspapers. It is in twenty-eight verses of six
lines each. The earliest reprint known to me is
that which appeared in the New York *Scottish
American* in 1859, on the occasion of the Burns
Centenary. It re-appeared in the *Truthseeker*,

edited by Rev. John Page Hopps, v. 12, p. 14,
January, 1875. From this it was copied into
The Scottish Exchange, No. 5, vol. 1, May 5, 1876.
(It seems also to have appeared in the New-
castle *Weekly Chronicle*, also in 1876 ?). In a
periodical called *Acadiensis*, a quarterly devoted
to the interests of the maritime provinces of
Canada, it again appears (v. 3, pp. 219-223), and
the authorship attributed to the Hon. James
Brown, Surveyor General of New Brunswick,
who was born in Forfarshire in 1790, emigrated
to Canada in 1808, and died in 1870. In a
biographical sketch of Brown, by Mr. D. F.
Maxwell, which appears in the same volume
(pp. 184-191), the author states that "The
original manuscript (!), with the author's
signature, and in his own handwriting, is now
in the possession of his descendants . . . . and
is thought to have been first written about 1857
or 1858." The production of the poem, Mr.
Maxwell goes on to say, "was no doubt inspired
by a prize competition offered by one of the
Scottish Societies for the best poem to com-
memorate the then approaching Burns Cen-
tennial. Many MSS. were contributed from
all over the world, and the judges to whom they
were referred found much difficulty in deter-
mining whether this poem should occupy first
or second place. It was decided, however, after
much deliberation, to award it second place. It
bore no authorship at the time, but purported to
have been written by ' His Satanic Majesty '
himself, from the ' Deil's Chair,' so called, a
somewhat famous spot near Lumleyden in

Forfarshire. . . . The reasons given by the author to his intimate friends for not appending his name are said to have been purely political ones. The poem first appeared in public print in America in the *Scottish American Journal*, in 1859, and the editor of that paper in a note appended said (in part) : ' What to do with this poem we have been at a loss to know. It has been under the editorial ban for twelve months. Too heterodox, some think, to print, but too good to lose. Of all the centenary poems which have been sent us, this is perhaps the cleverest ' " (p. 190). A copy of the poem, as published in *Acadiensis*, was said to have been sent to a brother of Mr. Brown, living near Dundee in 1903, who gave it to the *People's Journal*, and it appeared in that periodical as the work of the Hon. James Brown of New Brunswick ! Ditchburn's verses were also reprinted in Dr. J. D. Ross's *All About Burns*, New York [1896], pp. 123-126 ; and an edition in pamphlet form (8 pp., 12°) with an introductory note by A. Earnest Parry, was published in Kirkcaldy by John Davidson & Son, n.d. George Carter, in his *Lyric Homilies*, Glasgow, 1884, printed the first ten verses of Ditchburn with additions of his own.

THE DEIL'S ANSWER TO HIS VERA WORDY FRIEND R—— B——.

Tophet, 15th day of the Month Adar.
Quæ tibi, quæ tali, reddam, pro carmine dona ?
—Virg.

> For sic a Sang as I gat frae ye,
> My wordy Friend, what can I gie ye ?

[Ebenezer Picken, the author of this address and of " Verses on the death of Robert Burns," was born in Paisley in the year 1769, the son of a silk weaver of that town. He attended the classes in Glasgow University for several sessions and studied for the ministry, but his passion for poetry seriously interfered with the progress of his studies and caused him eventually to adopt the precarious professions of teacher and author.

In 1788 he published at Paisley a small volume of poems, subsequently in 1813 republished by subscription with many additions in two volumes. In April 1791 he delivered at the Pantheon, Edinburgh, an essay on the question " Whether have the exertions of Allan Ramsay or Robert Fergusson done more honour to Scottish poetry ? " in which he gave the pre-eminence to the former. Alexander Wilson, the Ornithologist, took the part of Fergusson. In the same year Picken accepted the position of schoolmaster at Falkirk, and there he married

Robina, daughter of the Rev. John Belfrage, minister of the Burgher Congregation. From Falkirk he went to Carron to accept the position of teacher in an endowed school, and there he remained until 1796. In this year he removed to Edinburgh, where he became manager in a mercantile house, and later began business on his own account with unfortunate results. It was during the hours of relaxation occasionally enjoyed in the midst of laborious industry, he states in the preface to his 1813 edition, that the greater part of the poems in that edition were produced. In his " Valediction " he says :

" Misfortune fell sae lang has kept
   My nose upo' the grunstane,
That, but for rhime, my heart wad break,
   Tho' 'twar as hard's a whunstane."

On the failure of his business he became a teacher of languages, but was harassed continually with poverty. At the end of his " Miscellaneous Poems " he advertises his " Pocket Dictionary of the Scottish Dialect " as " in the press and speedily will be published." It, however, did not appear until two years after his death, which occurred in 1816, and was a work of much service to Dr. Jamieson in the preparation of his supplementary two volumes published in 1825.]

So, zealous Robin ! stout an' fell,
True champion for the cause o' Hell ;
Thou beats the Righteous down, pell mell,
   Sae frank an' furthy,
That, o' a place whar Devils dwell,
   There's nane mair worthy.

Gif thou gang on the gait thou's gaun,
Ilk fearless Fiend sal by thee staun,
That bows aneath my high commaun :
      Sae be na frightit,
For I sal len' my helpin' haun,
      To see thee rightit.

Thou dis as weel's could be expeckit
O' ane, wha's wit lay lang negleckit ;
An' gets thy rank ideas deckit
      In rhime sae bra',
That thou's in Hell right well respeckit
      Amang us a'.

Sae fear'd I'm for the gospel gun,
To see my Friends I canna win ;
But tell sic chields as thee, my son,
      I'll see them sune ;
An' thee an' me's hae curious fun,
      Or a' be doon.

The Endor witch, wha liv'd lang syne,
Was a right honest friend o' mine ;
An' Haman, wha in tale sal shine,
      For zealous spite ;
But nane o' them did feats like thine,
      In black an' white.

Sae high as thee they coudna speel :
They coudna string a verse sae leal ;
Nor, on the standin' faith, sae weel
      Spue out their tauntins ;
Nor pen love letters to the Deil,
      To scrape acquaintance.

In trowth, thou has an unco knack
O' rhimin' skill, an' ready clack :
I wad me, Nature was na slack
    In makin' thee :
Thou has mair wit than the hail pack
    O' Deils like me.

Since on the earth we first took staunin',
We've ay been sae ta'en up wi' plannin',
An' plottin', that, keep me frae bannin' !
    The deil a styme
O' leisure can we hain for scannin'
    O' gleesome rhime.

Had I no read your line aff haun,
I'm sure I boost to let it staun ;
I'se wad, nae General in your laun
    Has sic a pine,
An' fash, wi a wanruly baun,
    As I've wi' mine.

Ilk hour, they mak' sic rout an' rair
Soun' thro' ilk region o' the air ;
They aft times mak' my heart sae sair,
    Sae fyk'd, an' flurried ;
War't possible, nae styme I care
    I'm dead an' buried.

I'm sure I whiles think I sal dee,
War't no, to pit mysel' in kee,
I raise a tempest on the sea,
    Or i' the air :
Or read some funny rhime frae thee,
    To drown my care.

There's no a Bard, alive e'enow,
That hits my taste sea weel as you ;
Some cantin' fowks, your rhimes, I trow,
        Ca' worthless blether ;
But, be na feard—ye'se get yer due,
        Whan we forgether.

Letnae their flirds an flytin' flee ye ;
For I'm resolv'd to come an' see ye,
" To spend an hour in daffin wi' ye,"
        An' taste thegither :
A Friend's advice I mean to gie ye,
        Just like a Brither.

Now Bob, my lad, cheer up thy saul :
In Goshen thou sal tent thy faul' ;
An', gin thou's ay as blyth an' baul',
        As I'm a Deil,
Thou'se no kick up, till thou's right aul' ;
        Sae, fare thee weel.

THE DEIL'S REPLY TO ROBERT BURNS.

By JAMES DITCHBURN.

[Nothing appears to be known about the author, and it is probable that "James Ditch-burn" is a pseudonym.]

O WAES me, Rab! hae ye gane gyte?
What is't that gars ye tak' delight
To jeer at me, and ban, and flyte,
    In Scottish rhyme,
And fausely gie me a' the wyte
    O' ilka crime?

O' auld nicknames ye hae a fouth,
O' sharp sarcastic rhymes a routh,
And as you're bent to gie them scouth,
    'Twere just as weel
For you to tell the honest truth,
    And shame the de'il.

I dinna mean to note the whole
O' your unfounded rigmarole,
I'd rather haud my tongue, and thole
    Your clishmaclavers,
Than try to plod through sic a scrole
    O' senseless havers.

O' warlocks and o' witches a',
O' spunkies, kelpies, great or sma',
There isna ony truth ava
    In what you say,
For siccan frichts I never saw
    Up to this day.

The truth is, Rab, that wicked men
When caught in crimes that are their ain,
To find a help are unco fain
    To share the shame,
And so they shout, wi' micht and main,
    " The de'il's to blame ! "

Thus I am blamed for Adam's fa'—
You say that I maist ruined a' ;
I'll tell ye ae thing, that's no twa,
    It's just a lee ;
I fasht na wi' the pair ava',
    But loot them be.

I'd nae mair haun in that transgression
You deem the source o' a' oppression,
And wae, and death, and man's damnation,
    Than you yersel' ;
I filled a decent situation
    When Adam fell.

And, Rab, gin ye'll just read your Bible
Instead o' blin' Jock Milton's fable,
I'll plank a croon on ony table
    Against a groat,
To fin' my name, you'll no' be able,
    In a' the plot.

Your mither, Eve, I kent her brawly ;
A dainty quean she was, and wally,
But destitute of prudence wholly,
    The witless hizzie,
Aye bent on fun, and whiles on folly
    And mischief busy.

Her Father had a bonnie tree,
The apples on't allured her e'e ;
He warned her no' the fruit to pree,
    Nor climb the wa',
For if she did, she'd surely dee,
    And leave it a'.

She didna do her father's biddin'—
She didna mind her husband's guidin' ;
Her ain braw hoose, she wadna bide in,
    But strayed awa,
Depending on her art o' "hidin'"
    To blin' them a'.

As for the famous serpent story
To lee I'd baith be shamed and sorry,
I'ts just a clever allegory,
    And weel writ doon,
The wark o' an Egyptian Tory—
    I ken the loon.

Your tale o' Job, the man o' Uz,
Wi' reekit claes and reested guiz,
My hornie hoofs and brocket phiz
    Wi' ither clatter,
Is maistly, after a' the bizz,
    A moonshine matter.

Auld Job, I kent the carle right weel,
An honest, decent, kintra chiel,
Wi' heid to plan an' heart to feel,
    And hand to gie—
He wadna wranged the verra De'il
    A brown bawbee.

The man was gey and weel to do,
Had horse, and kye, and ousen too,
And sheep, and stots, and stirks, enow
    To fill a byre ;
O' meat and claes, a' maistly new,
    His heart's desire.

Forby, he had within the dwellin's
Three winsome queans and five braw callans,
Ye wadna, in the hale braid lallans,
    Nae faund their marrow,
Were ye to search frae auld Tantallans
    To braes o' Yarrow.

It happened that three breekless bands
O' caterans came from distant lands,
And took what fell among their hands
    O' sheep and duddies,
Just like your reiven Hielan' clans
    Or Border bodies.

I tell ye, Rab, I had nae share
In a' the tulzie, here or there ;
I lookit on, I do declare,
    A mere spectator,
Nor said, nor acted, less or mair
    Aboot the matter.

Job had a minstrel o' his ain,
A genius rare, and somewhat vain
O' rhyme and lear—but then again,
    Just like yersel',
O' drink and lasses unco fain,
    The neer-do-weel.

He'd sing o' lads and ladies fair,
O' love and hope, and mirk despair,
And wondrous tales wad whiles prepare,
        And string thegither,
For a' he wanted was a hair
        To mak' a tether.

So with intention fully bent,
My doings to misrepresent,
That book o' Job he did invent ;
        And then his rhymes
Got published in Arabic print
        To suit the times.

You poets, Rab, are a' the same,
Of ilka kintra, age, and name,
Nae matter what may be your aim
        Or your intentions ;
Maist a' your characters o' fame
        Are pure inventions.

Shakespeare mak's ghaists an' witches plenty,
Jock Milton, deevils mair than twenty,
Tom Puck will soon be crouse and canty
        Wi' Rab the Ranter ;
And you yersel' are mair than vauntie
        O' " Tam o' Shanter."

Your dogs are baith debaters rare,
Wi' sense galore and some to spare,
While even the verra brigs o' Ayr
        Ye gar them quarrel—
Tak' Coila ben to deck your hair
        Wi' Scottish laurel.

Yet Robin, lad, for a' your spite,
And taunts, and jeers, and wrangfu' wyte,
I find, before you end your flyte
    And win' yer pirn,
Ye're nae sae cankered in the bite
    As in the girn.

For when ye think he's doomed to dwell
The lang for-ever-mair in hell,
Ye come and bid a kind farewell,
    And—guid be here—
E'en for the verra de'il himsel'
    Let fa' a tear.

And Rab, I'm just as wae for thee,
As ever thou cans't be for me ;
For less ye let the drink abee,
    I'll tak' my aith,
Ye'll a' gang wrang, and maybe dee
    A drunkard's death.

Sure as ye mourned the daisies' fate,
That fate is thine, nae distant date ;
Stern Ruin's plowshare drives elate
    Full on thy bloom,
And crushed beneath the furrow's weight
    May be thy doom.

EPISTLE TO MR. ROBERT BURNS.

[This Epistle appears in the *Scots Magazine*
for 1788, pp. 558-559. The initials signed at
the end, "J. J——n, F——r," certain allusions
in the poem itself, and the thorough knowledge
of the language displayed by the writer point, I
think, to Dr. John Jamieson, author of the
Etymological Dictionary of the Scottish Language,
as having been the author. Dr. Jamieson was
born in Glasgow in 1759, a few weeks after Burns,
and died in Edinburgh in 1838. He studied for
the ministry, and in 1781 was ordained minister
of the Antiburgher congregation of Forfar.
While a student at the university, he contributed
several pieces to Ruddiman's *Weekly Magazine*,
published poems on the "Sorrows of Slavery"
(1789) and on "The Water Kelpie," etc. It may
be mentioned, however, that some of the more
unusual or uncommon words occurring in the
poem are not listed in his *Dictionary*.]

FAIR fa' ye, honest rhyming Rab,
For a' your dainty weel-turn'd gab ;
It gars me claw as wi' the scab
        For very glee :
A plack mair than wi' ony knab
        I'd drink wi' thee.

Wha wu'd hae thought, a kintry chield,
That jumply had frae storm a bield,
And a' his days the yird had till'd,
      Sae cruse cou'd craw ?
Wi' ony menstral of your eild
      Ye'd shake a fa'.

For a' the bards that rais'd their sugh,
When aince ye yoke your sturdy pleuch,
Ye shaw there still is ground eneuch
      No yet ta'en in :
Awa' ye skreed, the wark tho' teuch,
      Thro' heath or whin.

Your ingine, like a coutter glib
That ev'ry weyward weed can snib,
Casts up—I wadna like to fib,
      Your verse sae trig,
It's to a weel-pleuch'd acre sib
      In fur and rigg.

But when ye tak your murd'ring pattle,
And summon ony chield to battle,
You len' him sic a vitious rattle,
      A mouse I'd be,
Far rather than that ye shou'd ettle
      Sick straiks at me.

Your Muse is sic a feckfu' beast,
She's no' like mine, aft gi'en to rieft,
Nor slacks the brecham on her breast,
      Nor needs she gaod ;
Tho' gin she sees a dand'ring priest,
      Sair snorts the yade.

Weel do I ken the banks of Ayr,
And Luggar's rocks, for I ha' there
Spent mony a day (and laucht at care) ;
      But syn I kent
That ye was near, I've rued fu' sair
      My time misspent.

And thoch I'm now richt sweir to budge,
To Coila's bony plains I'd trudge,
And a' my travel wadna grudge,
      Gin ye wad say't,
" Cum here and tak a pint hudgemudge : "
      For I'm but blate.

And thoch I'm fankit i' my tether,
And darna thole ilk kind o' weather,
That we micht hae a spell thegither
      A nicht or twae,
I'd leave the best bed made o' feather
      For ane o' strae.

Ae bard should stick like hand and gluve,
To ilka brither in true luve,
And ne'er let envy's ruthless hoove,
      Crush out its saul ;
But leal and honest ay should pruve,
      And ne'er divall.

We're a' like birds hatch'd in ae nest,
A lav'rock's ca't gin't fit you best :
Ane sings, like you, 'Boon a' the rest,
      And soars like th' eagle :
By weakness o' my pipe confess'd,
      I'm wally-draggle.

But yet ye manna tak it ill
That ony brither o' the quill
(Tho' he kythe little but guid-will)
     Gi's best advice,
Nor prance as gin ye'd gott'n a pill
     O' priming spice.

The wrig that near the ground man flutter,
Tho' naething but a feckless twitter,
May hear the greedy gled's dread clutter,
     And ane fu' hich
That soars, save frae a death right bitter
     Wi' its bit skriech.

And first, misken na bonny Jean,
Wha's ay, tho' haimly, dink and clean,
For ony glaiket town-bred quean,
     Wha tries attour ye
To cast the glamour o' her e'en
     Just to devour ye.

Wi' frizzled pow, like Blackamoor,
And plaister'd face, like some auld w——e,
And rump, as gin she gaed on four,
     Auld simple Nature,
To ken her scarce is't in thy pow'r
     For thy ain creature !

Your Maker's praise ye weel can sing
Whan aince ye twitch that pleasant string ;
And may your voice gar yon vau't ring,
     When here its gane !
But wi't a gude tune it man bring,
     Or twill hae nane.

The craw is herse upon a tree,
As weel's when craiking on the lee ;
The place nae change o' note can gie ;
      He's ay a craw :
Its craik is better heard on hie,
      And that is a'.

Tho' he could twitch yon starry lift,
It wadna gi'm a lav'rock's gift.
'T man surely then be our best thrift
      Richt notes to learn
While here ; we're cum to our last shift,
      Whan laid in cairn.

O'er mony a field I'se warn ye've stottit,
Whan cum the seed-time Heav'n allottit :
But tell me, hae na ye ever notit
      The seed that grew
The sam' be't soon or late ye got it,
      Wi that ye sew ?

Ye've aften seen the weel-fill'd hap
Its rough seed cast in earth's wide lap ;
But did ye ever ken it hap
      That frae its seed
A pear-tree rais'd its flow'ry tap
      And its fruit gi'ed ?

Your metre weel eneuch wad scan,
Tho' ye did neither curse nor ban,
It looks na weel in ony man
      That name to skaith
By whilk the very breath is drawn
      That forms ane aith.

And gin ye really trow the Bible,
However mickle ye sou'd scribble,
Ne'er like ane allevoly fribble,
  Gi' it a sneer ;
There's fouk eneuch at it to nibble,
  Tho' bards keep clear.

Waesuck ! there's little made by scoffin,
Death puts an end to a' sic daffin ;
Whan you or I are laid in coffin,
  But ill 'twould tell,
Gin fowk shou'd say, " there lies a ruffian
  That laucht at h—l."

Your forbeir, wha in Salem sang,
Tho' aft he gaed e'en richt far wrang,
(And wha's bot failings men amang ?)
  And aft ill-feated,
Ne'er into scorner's chair wad bang ;
  Sick wark he hated.

And tho' frae some fouk ye may differ,
(Wha wadna like wi' you to niffer)
Than's needfu' thinking them far stiffer,
  To fill their shoon
Ye'd aiblins twin wi' your best heifer
  Or a' be done.

Their lack o' charity ye blame,
" 'Gainst them as hypocrites exclaim,
Wha sic a life as yours condemn :
  But some are grudging
That ye are tarr'd as thick as them
  The heart in judging.

There's mony wha to faith lay claim,
Whose lives wou'd put gude warks to shame,
But their faith is na worth the name,
  Its a' presumption :
Yet to like faith, the waur for them,
  Wou'd kythe sma' gumshon.

True faith and warks are sib to ither
And where sincere gang ay thegither ;
But ye man mind that Faith's the mither
  And Warks the weans.
As lang as ye about this swither,
  Ye lose your pains.

'Cause sum fouk winna curse nor drink
Its e'en richt hard that ye shou'd think,
They do as ill when ithers wink :
  The pruif's fair striding,
Whan ye man flee, to fill a chink,
  To " th'art o' hiding."

Vou man ! ye at the clergy bicker,
As gin ye'd sworn a league fu' sicker,
And sign'd it wi' your heart's red liquor
  A' theirs to spill.
Ane maist wad think sum kintry vicar
  Had us'd ye ill.

Ye've aiblins sat the cuttie-stool
For some bit brat that cust the hule,
And, like a calf, there dried sic dule,
  As left you wishing
Yourself a stot, tho' else a snull
  But in priest pushing.

Auld Cloots and you are unco cosh,
To him ye mak your tale as tosh
As gin ye'd drunk out o' ae dush
      Till ye were kedgy ;
Or cheek for chow held up your gash
      At Mass John's dredgy.

But in your lug tho' he be bizzin
That ye're his weel beloved cousin,
And bid ye heart'ly weet your wizen
      And lauch at doom ;
He'll neither hear your rhyme nor reason,
      Your glass when tum.

E'en now he's lauchin in his sleeve
Sae carelesslie to see you scrieve,
And that yoursell ye sou'd believe
      Sae wondrous supple
As jink him, or 'bout his reprieve
      Indulge ae scruple.

And as your luve to him's nae sma',
And weel ye like the lasses bra',
Tak tent, his claim to th' haill to shaw
      And stap a' quarrels,
He dinna pu' your nizz awa
      By way o' arrils.

Your " Cottar's night " agrees nae weel
Wi' your epistill to the Deill ;
And diff'rent qualms ye seem to feel
      When Death cums near ye,
Than whan to Holy fair ye reel
      Wi' scoffs to cheer ye.

If something tells ye a's nae richt,
And gies ye now and then a fricht,
Be sure its warnings dinna slicht ;
    The house dividit
Against itsell is far frae ticht ;
    Ye canna hide it.

Tho' wi' a winze a priest commend
And by the slump you praises send,
Wha e'en sum gude advice sou'd lend,
    Yet ye man mind,
Its nae the first time we hae kend
    Blind lead the blind.

Frae hally book we only hear
Of ae priest who begoud to swear ;
Nor was he in his aiths, I fear,
    Sair to be trustit :
It cost him mony a richt saut tear
    Or he o'ercust it.

Your conscience ye may gie to keep
To sicklike fouk to help its sleep,
And think me but a "gouket sliep "
    And scorn ane answer :
But dinna haud that friend o'er cheap,
    Who dares to censure.

F——r.   J. J——n.

VERSES, WRITTEN IN BROAD SCOTCH AND ADDRESSED TO ROBERT BURNS, THE AIRSHIRE POET.

[These verses appear in *The Literary Magazine and British Review*, v. 2, pp. 297-298, London, 1789. In a footnote the Editor says :—
" These verses were published some time ago in a London newspaper ; but as we have been favoured with a correct copy of them from the author, we flatter ourselves that they will not be unacceptable to our numerous and respectable subscribers in the North."]

FAIR fa' you, Robie, canty callan,
Wha rhym'st amaist as weel as Allan
And pleasest Highland lads and lawlan',
  Wi' your auld gab
May never wae come near your dwallin'
  Nor skaith nor scab.

I've read your warks wie muckle glee,
Auld Lucky Nature there I see,
Has gie'n you genius like a bee,
  To suck the flowers,
Where'er ye gang weel may ye be,
  Blythe be your hours.

Let college sumphs glib Horace praise,
Gie auld blin Homer still the bays,
And about Virgil mak a phrase,
    A gude Scotch taste
Prefers your ain untutor'd lays
    To a' their best.

Let them like gouks auld Latin speak,
And blether out their brak-jaw Greek,
Tho' ye was born where hills are bleak,
    And cauld winds bla,
And tho' frae biuks nae helps ye seek
    Ye ding them a'.

May independence be you lot,
To gar your musie frisk and trot,
And may ye never want a groat
    To drown your care,
When ye put on your Sunday's coat,
    To rant or fair.

When lavrocks tune their bonny throats,
And i' the lift pour forth their notes,
When bleating ewes first leave their cots,
    And climb the braes,
While round her dam each lamie trots
    And frisks and plays.

O ! Rab, it's pleasant then to stray
Where little burnies steal away,
And hazles shield frae Phebus' ray,
    And muse and think,
And while the breesies round ane play
    Mak versies clink.

Aft man—but, ah, these days are gane,
Have I thus stoited a' alane,
Or sat upon a foggy stane
        Beneath a brae.
Whar Philomel has made her mane
        And sung her wae.

From rural scenes I've lang been torn,
And mony a skelp frae fortune borne,
Lamenting that of life's gay morn,
        I'm now bereft.
I see no rose, but find the thorn
        Alane is left.

O! man when years hing o'er the back,
And bend us like a muckle pack,
Life then will scarce be worth a plack,
        For mirth and glee,
To younger swankies in a crack
        Frae us will flee.

Auld Time, that jinking slippery chiel,
Ere lang will make us end our reel,
And a' our fire and spirits queel,
        And quench the low,
That now within our breasts we feel,
        And bleach our pow.

Let us the present hour then seize,
And reckon gain what the niest gies,
It's vain for what nane o' us sees,
        Our heads to fash,
Or yet to let the world teize,
        Us wi' its trash.

Cou'd I, O! Rob, but brak my tether,
And ony whare wi' you forgether,
I'm sure we'd souple baith our leather,
        I'd pawn my lugs,
We'd mak our hearts as light's a feather
        Wi' reaming jugs.

FAMILIAR EPISTLE TO ROBIE BURNS, THE PLOWMAN POET, IN HIS OWN STYLE.

BY THE REV. JOHN SKINNER.

[The Rev. John Skinner was born at Balfour, Aberdeenshire, on the 3rd of October, 1721. Originally destined for the Presbyterian ministry, he became an Episcopalian, and in 1742 was appointed to the charge of Langside, where he ministered for sixty-four years. As a consequence of the Jacobite rebellion in 1746, the lot of the Episcopalians was a hard one, and Skinner, though not a Jacobite, suffered severely. He published an *Ecclesiastical History of Scotland* (2 v., 1788) and some controversial writings, but is best remembered by his songs, particularly "Tullochgorum," which Burns declared to be "the best Scotch song ever Scotland saw." He died 16th June, 1807, in his son's house. In the introduction to Skinner's *Amusement of leisure hours; or poetical pieces chiefly in the Scottish dialect* (Edinburgh, 1809), the editor gives the following account of the origin of this Epistle :

"On his arrival at Aberdeen, Mr. Burns having called on Mr. Chalmers, the printer, our Author's son happened to meet him on the stair of the printing-office, and having accompanied him into an adjoining room, was much entertained by an hour's conference on several very interesting topics. Of this interview he wrote a particular account to his father, mentioning also how much Burns regretted that he did not know where *Linshart* lay, as he would have gone twenty miles out of his way to have seen the Author of *Tullochgorum*. This compliment produced an acknowledgment, under the title of a ' *Familiar Epistle to Robie Burns, the Plowman Poet, in his own style.*' The following account of it appears in a letter to Miss Margaret Chalmers (now Mrs. Hay of Edinburgh) in Cromek's ' *Reliques of Robert Burns,*' &c. lately published, where he says :—' I got an excellent poetic epistle yesternight from the old venerable Author of Tullochgorum, John of Badenyon, &c. I suppose you know he is a clergyman. It is by far the finest poetic compliment I ever got. I will send you a copy of it.' "

Skinner's Epistle is also published in *Miscellanea Perthensis*, Perth, 1801, and in the reprint of this work published in London under the title of *The Pic Nic, a miscellany of prose and verse*, 1802.]

O HAPPY hour for evermair,
That led my chill up *Cha'mers'* stair,
And gae him, what he values sair,
        Sae braw a skance
Of Ayrshire's dainty Poet there,
            By lucky chance.

Wae's my auld heart I was na wi' you,
Tho' worth your while I could na gie you :
But sin' I had na hap to see you,
    Whan ye was north,
I'm bauld to send my service to you,
    Hyne o'er the Forth.

Sae proud's I am, that ye heard
O' my attempts to be a Bard,
And think my muse nae that ill-fawrd,
    Seil o' your face !
I wadna wish for mair reward
    Than your guid grace.

Your bonny beukie, line by line,
I've read, and think it freely fine ;
Indeed, I winna ca't divine,
    As others might :
For that, ye ken, frae pen like mine,
    Wad no be right.

But, by my sang, I dinna wonner,
That ye've admirers mony hun'er ;
Let gowkit fleeps pretend to skunner,
    And tak offence,
Ye've naething said that lcuks like blun'er,
    To fowk o' sense.

Your pauky " Dream " has humour in't ;
I never saw the like in print.
The Birth-day Laurit durst na' mint,
    As ye hae dane ;
And yet there's nae a single hint
    Can be ill ta'en.

Your " Maillie," and your " Auld Mare,"
And " Hallow-even's " funny cheer—
There's nane that reads them far nor near
      But reezes Robie ;
And thinks them as diverting gear
      As Yorrick's Tobie.

But o' the well-tauld " Cottar's Night "
Is what gies me the maist delight—
A piece sae finish'd and sae tight,
      There's nane o's a'
Cou'd preachment timmer cleaner dight
      In kirk or ha'.

But what needs this or that to name ?
It's own'd by a' there's nae a theme
Ye tak in hand, but's a' the same :
      And nae ane o' them,
But weel may challenge a' the fame
      That we can gie them.

For me, I heardly allow you
The warld of praise sae justly due you ;
And but a *Plowman !* sall I trow you ?
      Gin it be sae,
A miracle I will avow you,
      Deny't wha may !

Sae, what avails a leash o' lair
Thro' sev'n lang years, and some guid mair,
Whan *Plowman* lad, wi' nature bare,
      Sae far surpasses
A' we can do wi' study sair
      To climb Parnassus ?

But thanks to praise, ye're i' your prime,
And may chant on this lang, lang, time ;
For lat me tell you, 'tware a crime
    To had your tongue.
Wi' sic a knack's ye hae at rhyme,
    And ye sae young.

Ye ken, it's nae for ane like me
To be sae droll as ye can be,
But ony help that I can gie,
    Tho't be but sma',
Your least command, I'se lat you see
    Sall gar me draw.

An hour or sae, by hook and crook,
And may be twa, some orrow ouk,
That I can spare frae haly beuk,
    For that's my hobby,
I'll slip awa' to some bye neuk,
    And crack wi' Robie.

Wad ye but only crack again,
Just what ye like, in ony strain,
I'll tak it kind ; for, to be plain,
    I do expect it :—
And mair than that, I'll no be fain
    Gin ye neglect it.

To Linshart, gin my hame ye speir,
Where I hae heft near fifty year,
'Twill come in course, ye need na fear,
    The part's weel kent ;
And postage, be it cheap or dear,
    I'll pay content.

Now, after a', hae me exquees'd
For wissing nae to be refees'd ;
I dinna covet to be reez'd
    For this feel lilt.
But feel, or wise, gin ye be pleas'd,
    Ye're welcome till't.

Sae, canty Plowman, fare ye weel,
Lord bless you lang wi' hae and heil,
And keep you ay the honest chiel
    That ye hae been ;
Syne lift you till a better beil
    Whan this is dane !

P.S.

This auld Scot's muse I've courted lang,
    And spar'd nae pains to win her ;
Dowf tho' I be in rustic sang,
    I'm no a raw beginner.
But now auld age taks dowie turns,
    Yet, troth, as I's a sinner,
I'll ay be fond of Robie Burns
    While I can sign—John Skinner.

LINSHART, 25*th September*, 1787.

EPISTLE TO MR. ROBERT BURNS.

[This Epistle, which appears in the *Scots Magazine* for 1788, p. 608, is signed, J. R——d. Nothing more is known of the author.]

O FAM'D an' hi' renowned Rabbie,
Nane after thee may shaw his gabie,
Bit yet my muse, tho' unco shabby,
    Wad fain be in,
To shaw the frolics o' a' baby,
      Wi' wanton din.

She disna' mean to lord it o'er ye,
Or frae the list o' poets score ye,
For a' o' auld or modern story,
    Ye tak the lead ;
She hum'ly therefor dis implore ye
    To hear her creed.

Your braw epistles fan I read,
They gar me smile an' claw my head,
To think that ane, in kintry bred,
    Wi' little lear',
Wha at a pleugh-tail earns his bread,
    Sud craw sae clear.

Your verse fu' sleek it glides alang,
Wi' canty glee and cheerfu' clang,
Sublime ideas ye mix amang
        Your orat'ry,
That gars it hae a finer chang
        In poetry.

Wi' Homer great thee I compare,
For fancie's mood ye shaw fu' fair,
O' Horace wit ye want nae skair,
        To glibe awa',
Gars gouks like us baith gape an' stare,
        An' clap our paw.

The rural scenes ye paint so fine,
In fairest hue the colours shine ;
An' mony ither things the Nine
        Has stor'd ye wi',
That deeper o' Parnassian Wine
        Nane mayna pri'.

Bit here, my friend, I'm at a stand,
Whilk way to lend my helpin' hand,
Gin I your pleugh had i' my land,
        I'd ablins till,
An' ans'er ilka hard demand
        O' priest or d—l.

Wi' Clergymen ye're fairly out,
I read, wi' them ye've ha'en a bout,
For ane has lent you sic a rout,
        I see in print,
That frae the blaw ye've cause to lout,
        An' tak' good tent.

Bit o' their censures ha'e nae fear,
Ye ken fat sud fa' to your share,
If i' your breast ye penance bear,
  For ony crime,
It dis the burden much impair
  O' misspent time.

If e'er the D——l wis in wi' you,
'Twas very right to gi'm his due,
Gin't may be ca'd a fau't, for now
  I kenna better,
Bit deep philosophy you shew
  Into the matter.

'Bout modes o' faith fouk needna fike,
Lat ilk ane follow fat they like,
An' he that thinks he's free to speak,
  Maun get his will,
If ill proceeds, his mou' lat's steek
  Wi' Reason's bill.

Fat else is in Religion's view,
But to mak faithfu', good, an' true,
Fat conscience dictates for to do
  Is,—fat we can,
The leave trust to Him wha' kens how
  To help ilk man.

I'm blythe to find ye are nae quaker,
Modern religious hum-drum cracker,
Nor pedant, pedagogue, nor hawker
  In politics,
Sick like, nae scroundel hallanshaker
  Can shaw his tricks.

Like Patie Pindar ye can whistle,
An' shaw they're fools for a' their bustle,
Nae genty knight o' the Scots Thistle
      Ye need envy ;
While at the pleugh ye tug an' wirstle,
      Bid them good-bye.

If e'er a simmer's day I see,
I'll tak' a trip to your kintry,
An' gin ye i' the body be
      Expect that I'll come,
For well I ken your charity,
      Will mak' me welcum'.

                  J. R——d.

EPISTLE TO ROBERT BURNS, THE AYRSHIRE POET.

[These verses appeared in the *Edinburgh Evening Courant* for December 12, 1786, within a fortnight of the Poet's arrival in Edinburgh. They are understood to have been written by David Ramsay, printer of the *Courant*, and show a great familiarity with the Doric. They were reprinted in *The British Chronicle, or Union Gazette*, December, 29, 1786.]

WEEL, Rab, I conn'd a' o'er your beuk,
As I sat i' the ingle neuk
Yestreen, nor coost a sidelin' look,
    I was sae keen ;
Nor pried my gill, nor bannock breuk,
      Till a' was deen.

And, by my saul, ye are a wag
May Fergusson or Ramsay brag,
Ye jog awa' your aiver nag
    At a bra' lilt ;
But criesh o' whip or prickle jag
      To had her til't.

Whar win ye, man ?   Gin one may spier :
Our Embrugh fouk say ye're at Ayr,
Lord, lad, gif I could meet ye there,
    Tho' few my placks,
Ane o' *Sir Willie's notes* I'd ware
      Upo' your cracks.

Or should you this way cast your louman,
An' shaw yoursel' in likeness human,
Ye'd prove to College hashes' view, man,
    A sair affliction,
The Prince of Poets an' o' Ploughmen
    Nay lyin' fiction.

Ye say ye are a wat-mow'd birkie,
And wi' the lasses play at smirkie ;
My fegs ! Ye'll fin' nae better dirkie
    Than thae same twa ;
To lay ye yavil, like a stirkie
    Choak'd i' the sta'.

Tak tent, ye loon, be nae sae baul',
O' Mah'met's fare to hae a haul,
Tho' rife o' spunk, an' soun' in spaul,
    Ca' nae o'er fast—
The can that gangs aft to the wall
    Will crack at last.

Poor Fergusson ! I ken'd him weel,
He was a blythsome canty chiel ;
" I've seen him roun' the bickers reel "
    An' lilt his sang,
An' crack his joke, sae pat an' leal,
    Ye'd ne'er thought lang.

O had ye seen, as I hae seen him,
When nae " Blue Devils " did pervene him
An' heard the pipe the Lord had gi'en him
    In Scottish air,
Ye'd aiblins for an angel taen him,
    He sang sae rare.

But when by these d——d fiends attacket,
His fine-spun saul they hew'd an' hacket,
Your very heart-strings wad hae cracket
    To've seen him than ;
He was just like a headless tacket
    In shape o' man.

Eh, Rab, he was like mony ane,
Wha get a pund, they'll tak' a stane ;
He had a spark frae Phœbus gi'en,
    But, ah ! waes wow !
It bleaz'd up like a comet keen,
    An' burnt his pow.

Alas ! this is o'er douf a spring
For you, to hear, or me to sing ;
In troth, I fin' I'm no the thing
    Whan thinkan o' him,
Sae, sin' he's gane, may the Great King
    Great mercy show him.

An' now, my honest cock, fareweel,
Lang may ye ca' your rhiming wheel,
An' whan your bluid begins to jeel
    An' shanks grow fozie,
May Abram's bosom be your biel
    To had you cozie.

TO MR. BURNS, ON HIS POEMS.

[Of James Mylne, the author of this sympathetic and appreciative Epistle to Burns, but little appears to be known beyond the fact that he was laird of Lochill or Loch-hill, a small estate near Prestonpans, Haddingtonshire.   His son, George Mylne, in the preface to his father's volume, says : " His genius led him in an early period of life to poetry ; and his taste in that line of composition was afterwards cultivated and improved by a regular and liberal academical education, and an acquaintance with the best ancient and modern poets."   From an " Ode to Mr. H. D.," Mylne appears to have received part of his education at the Grammar School of Dalkeith, and from the dedication to Henry Dundas of Melville he appears to have been intimate with that nobleman from early youth. He died at Lochill on the 9th December, 1788. Burns was consulted by the Rev. Peter Carfrae, of Morham Manse, as to the best means of publishing Mylne's Poems, and in a letter dated Ellisland, March 1789, gave his opinion as to the best way to go about the matter.   From an allusion in his letter to Mr. Carfrae it would appear that the Epistle here printed, was the last poetical piece written by Mylne.   Mylne's " Poems, consisting of miscellaneous pieces, and two tragedies," were published in Edinburgh by William Creech in 1790.   Eight hundred and thirty-five individuals, including " Mr. Robert Burns, Ellisland," subscribed for ten hundred and ninety-nine copies of the work.]

On yon green sod what maiden sits,
   Wi' garland dow'd, and looks forlorn !—
Lord keep the lassie in her wits !
   She sings, and yet she seems to mourn !
Do ye no ken the Scottish muse ?
   Here aft she seeks her darling shade ;
And aft wi' tears that grave bedews,
   Where poor *Rob Ferguson* was laid.

But whisht ! she speaks ?—" My dearest callan,
   A fair stroke was thy death to me !
For, since I lost my winsome *Allan*,
   My only hope was sheught in thee ?
Nae mair our verses, smooth and strang,
   Our men to martial fame incite :
Or warbled in melodious sang,
   Our maidens melt wi' fast delight.

" Our language, banish'd now frae court,
   (For Scotland has nae court at hame)
Is lightly'd by the better sort ;
   And ilka coof main mimic them.
New-fangled fools gade to the South,
   And brought frae court new-fashion'd frazes,
That gar our auld anes sound uncouth ;
   And ev'n our mother's words bombaze us.

" Affected soplings feinzie shame
   Of ilka thing benorth the Tweed ;
But whe wad fash their head wi' them !
   The blockheads scarce a word can read."
" Ged tak me, Mem, I kennot read
   " Thees your owld-fashion'd vulgar Scotch ! "
" Half Scots, half English, they proceed,
   " Smashing baith tongues to base hotch potch.

" We flatter thus a friend, when braw,
  " And cringe to him when gear is sent him ;
" But when his back is at the wa',
  " We blush to own that e'er we kent him.
" I little thought ance in a day,
  " When our ain bards sae sweetly sung,
" That glossaries we boot to hae,
  " To teach Scots men their native tongue.

" Or that our sangs, sae peerless good,
  " Thro' this false taste, this pride new-fangled,
" Boot be, to mak them understood,
  " In *English versions*,* vilely mangled.
" Afore he wrote, bauld *Ramsay* saw
  " The smeddom o' our tongue decay ;
" His words, as if caukt on a wa',
  " Were wearing fainter ilka day.

" Yet he in nature's genuine strains
  " Our feelings sae distinctly draws,
" He'll ever on his native plains,
  " And foreign too, command applause.
" Our dying tongue, by him reviv'd,
  " At *Allan's* death again grew faint :
" Till thou, my *Ferguson !* arriv'd,
  " And seem'd frae heav'n ance errant sent.

" To teach the warld that simple lays,
  " In nature's language, reach the heart ;
" And frae true genius get the praise
  " Deny'd to stiff refining art.—
" But *Robin's* sp'rit at last is here,
  " Wi' pleasure smiling on his brow !—
" Whare ha' ye been, gin ane may speer ?
  " And what maks ye sae blyth, **my dow** ? "

*See Ward's Gentle Shepherd.

" When wand'ring between Ayr and Doon,
  " I saw a laddie at the pleugh ;
" But Muse ! a sang I heard him crune,
  " That still seems in my lugs to sough."

" Fallow mortal ! why sae hastie ;
  " Banish terror frae thy breastie ;
" Wae's me for the chance that chac'd thee
  " Frae thy snug housie."
" Twas some that way ; and addrest to
  " A till'd-up mousie.

" He loos'd his pleugh.   I rade wi' him
  " On his auld white mare, sonsie Maggie ;
" Wha, proud to think she'd live in rhime,
  " Cockt head and tail, like ony staiggie.
" I lookt into his breast, and saw
  " Compassion for his fallow-creature,
" Amang the feelings, ane and a',
  " That maist embellish human nature.

" I look'd up into his head—
  " Gude losh !—What bright poetic fancies !
" A' striving whilk shou'd hae the lead,
  " In soon-intended rhiming dances.
" True judgment there directed a',
  " And let them out in proper order ;
" Imagination buskt them braw ;
  " And memory sat clark-recorder.

" The virtues a' to recommend
    " Meetly appear'd their common aim ;
" But their true motive (weel I kend)
    " Was ardour for poetic fame.
" I saw them plan, in calked lines,
    " Some sleely-jibing admonitions,
" To drive our dour, dull Scots divines
    " Frae gloomy, canting superstitions.

" I saw them plan the *Cottar's ingle :*
    " Where happy sat man, wife, lass, callan ;
" And, in the general joy to mingle,
    " Ev'n hawkie routs ayont the hallan.
" Frae hawkie comes the halesome feast,
    " On which well-pleas'd they sup or dine ;
" And in thae sober draughts maist blest,
    " They never think of costly wine.

" Cracks, tales, and sangs, them canty keep,
    " Till th' hours bring wonted bed-time roun' ;
" Then sound on caff or strae they sleep,
    " While gentles, sleepless, fret on down.
" Blush, Greatness, at your ill-spent time !
    " To you such bliss is seldom given.
" Can ye conceive the thoughts sublime,
    " On which they rise frae earth to heaven ?

" Ablins the while your groveling thoughts
    " Are some infernal purpose brewing,
" To turn them frae their peacefu' cotts,
    " Or a' their peace, and *Jenny*, ruin.*
" Thae fancies, when they wad befriend
    " The poor folk, flow in fast succession ;
" And when harsh masters they wad bend,
    " Their very tykes bark at oppression.

*An allusion to Burns's poem of the Cottar's Saturday night.

" They'll sing in hamely pastoral stile,
  " (For which nae nation e'er cou'd brag us),
" Sangs that will aye gar Scotland smile
  " At whisky, or a good fat haggies.
" In soothing, sympathising strain,
  " They shall revive the heart that mourns."
" Then cried the Muse, a' fidging fain,
  " I see you've found my *Robbie Burns !*

" He frae his birth has been my care !
  " He, till he dies shall be the same ;
" And sangs frae him ye'll shortly hear,
  " To rival yours, and *Ramsay's* fame."

Then crew the cock.   The vision fled.
And whare was I ?—just in my bed !
The dream ay fistling in my head,
        I cou'd na rest ;
But to write this to *Burns,* I said,
        I'll do my best.

My best !—Alake !—Write *Burns !*—O fy !
What is there *Burns* can ken me by ?
Though sometimes in the Muse's pye
        I've had a finger,
I've only shown, I fear, that I
        Am nae great singer.

For had the few lines I hae penn'd,
Been worth, they had been better kenn'd.
Conscious mysel they'd thole amend,
        I ne'er durst print them ;
But wore them in my pouch t' an end,
        Or brunt or tint them.

E

Yet I commend your nobler daring,
That, spite of critics and their jarring,
Cou'd bring to light your lines auld-farran,
        That mak sic din ;
And they've brought gowd to you I'se warran,
        In gowpens in.

I ken ye dinna care a snuff
For a' the silly fleeching stuff,
Wi' which the like o' me now puff
        Ye in presumption ;
For, though few bards be flattery-proof,
        Ye've rummle-gumption.

But Lord man !   tell me, how is't wie ye,
When ilka great man that ye see
Hads out his hand, or jouks to thee ?
        Are n' ye sae fain
Ye're like to swelt ?—I'm sure wer't me,
        'Twad turn my brain !

Yes, cock (as weel ye may) your crest,
And prize the praises o' the best !
But tent this :—Feather now your nest,
        Hain for a sair foot.
Syne ye may dine, when some o' the rest
        Maun lick the hare foot.

Ramsay at first, an' 'twas his due,
Was courted, prais'd, carest, like you :
That sangs and poets please maist when new,
        He wisely kend ;
And still made sangs, an' jeesies too,
        And siller hain'd.

Forgot, when auld, (I mind mysell)
He liv'd upon the Castle-hill,
Scarce ane e'er speer'd whare he did dwell,
        Or aught about him.
But what car'd *Allan?* He cou'd bell
        The cat without them.

Sae prudence bids you business chuse,
And no trust a' thing to the muse.
O'er aft we've seen the jilt misuse
        The best o' poets ;
And mak them fain to pawn their hose,
        For flip-flap diets.

Soon as his friends wi' praise inflame
The youthfu' bard to flee at fame,
Quite spoilt for ilka ither game,
        His thoughts tak flight,
And leave his cares, affairs, and hame,
        Clean out o' sight.

The gowd of a' thae parts far east,
Whare spite of fame, health, conscience, rest,
E'en ne'er-do-wells soon fill their kist,
        Affects him little ;
In poetry he to ding the best,
        Plys a' his mettle.

The live-lang day his sangs he'll crune,
To th' burnie or the breeze's tune ;
But finds, when near life's afternoon,
        He's a' wud wrang :
His shoon, hose, sark, breeks, a' thing done,
        Except his sang.—

It sets me weel to gie advice !
Have I mysell been aye sae wise ?
My game, when I threw lucky dice,
    Have I ne'er sticket ?
What have I made my words to splice ?
    Made ?—Deil be licket.

I've seen some wha begoud wi' less,
On whase head few lay muckle stress,
Wi' sheep and runts stock, blads o' grass ;
    While I hae nathing,
But meat, drink, health, content, and peace,
    And fire and claithing.

The wyte, when I lay on the muse,
She tells me aye, hersel t'excuse,
That I was ne'er sae gair as those
    Wham wit ca's dull.
Ye'll see, quo' she, spite o' your nose,
    Wha's been maist fool.

I hope ye think na to bespatter ye,
Like mony mae wi' fulsome flattery,
Far less to rouse your anger's battery,
    Was my intent.
To let ye ken I'd like to clatter wi' ye,
    Was a' I meant.

I seldom cringe to wealth or fame,
Or o' their friendship count the name ;
For the maist feck I live at hame,
    A farmer douce,
Amang my bairnies and their dame,
    In this thackt house.

Whare we'd be glad to see ye, Gabbie!
Fine fair I winna hecht.   No n' a' be,
Although we shou'd hae but ae sybie,
          Ye'se get your skair.
We'll aye get sa't to it ; and may be,
          Can barrow mair.

I downa bide to hear a glutton
Fraising about fine beef and mutton ;
I never ken or care a button
          What I'm to get ;
But leave the wife her will to put on
          The pat or spit.

The host dislikt, nae sumptuous fare,
Nae ven'son, turtle, or sic ware,
Wi' wines maist costly, rich, and rare,
          Which bring some guests,
Shou'd e'er mak me green to come near
          Him or his feasts.

My mind in this ye partly see.—
Gif ye dislike it, let it be.—
But gif it chance to please, and ye
          Think it worth while,
Eastward frae Edinbrugh by the sea,
          But fourteen mile ;

Ride through the town o' Prestonpans ;
Three miles ayont that leave the sands ;
Then ither twa thro' gude rich lands,
          You'll find Loch-hill,
And, ready to rin at your commands,
          Your friend
                              JAMES MYLNE.

ONE OF THE SHEPHERDS OF GALLOWAY
TO ROBERT BURNS,
AUTHOR OF SCOTTISH POEMS.

[The Rev. James Cririe, M.A., author of the following address, was born at New Abbey, Kirkcudbrightshire, April, 1752, and died in 1835. In his boyhood he was employed as a herd laddie. Like his contemporary, Alexander Murray, he was fond of study, became an able linguist, antiquary, and Latin Secretary to the Society of Antiquaries of Scotland. He began his career as a schoolmaster, and was successively Master of the Grammar Schools of Wigtown and Kirkcudbright, and Rector of the High School at Leith. In 1795 he became one of the Masters of the Edinburgh High School in succession to William Cruikshank, the Poet's friend. He was presented to the parish of Dalton, Dumfriesshire, in 1801 and held that charge till his death in 1835. In a letter to Peter Hill, 1st October, 1788, Burns dwells at length on Cririe's " Address to Loch Lomond," which he considered fully equal to Thomson's " Seasons." " Scottish scenery : or, Sketches in verse, descriptive of scenes chiefly in the Highlands of Scotland," London, 1803, was his only publication. This address occurs on pp. 317-328.]

FRAE southern shores, let Mauchline's bard
    Accept this gratulation :
Lang may sic wale o' sense be heard
    Frae men in humble station :

While foreign airs and lofty lays
 Suit only connoiseurs,
Sic witty rhymes, in hameo'er phrase,
 Can glad our heather muirs.
Hail ! honest Burns, thy wildest flight
 Excites our admiration,
And gies the heart sic true delight
 'Tis maist like inspiration.
Thy honest *Dogs,* sagacious brutes,
 They're baith well worth their dinner,
They've (shame gae by their sonsy snouts !)
 Mair sense nor mony a sinner.
Thy little *Louse,* thy *Halyfair,*
 And eke auld *Hallowe'en,*
The farmer's bony auld *White Mare,*
 Besides thy Wauking Dream ;
But chief o'er a' *The Cottar,*—warm—
 Sincere in his devotions :
May Heav'n protect thee safe frae harm,
 For sic aulfarrant notions !
May lasses a' get Burns by rote ;
 His lines sae smooth and easy ;
Nor *Mouse* nor *Maily* be forgot,
 Nor yet the *Mountain Daisy.*—
But wad ye ken what sort o' chiel
 Writes a' this lang win't blether ?
He's ane wha aft has sought a bield
 Wi' plaid and dog amang the heather ;
Has follow'd pleugh and harrow baith,
 Has helpet aft to win a kirn ;
For angry look though fear'd as death,
 Has sometimes thol'd a fremmit girn :
Though nouther fond o' whisky punch,
 Nor yet o' barmy liquor,

He never looks wi' sullen glunch
  On sic as bend the bicker :
Fond of a beuk, though late at night,—
  Fond of a friend to chat the gither :
Poor silly, luckless, thriftless wight,
  He thinks himsel your very brither.

EPISTLE ADDRESSED TO ROBERT BURNS.

By RICHARD GALL.

[Richard Gall was born at Linkhouse, near Dunbar, in December, 1776. At the age of eleven years he was apprenticed as a carpenter to his maternal uncle, but the occupation being uncongenial he gave it up and went to Edinburgh where his parents were then residing. Here he became an apprentice to David Ramsay, the proprietor of the *Edinburgh Evening Courant*. He died after a lingering illness in 1801. His collected poems and songs with a memoir by Alexander Balfour were published in Edinburgh in 1819.* His "Epistle addressed to Robert Burns" occurs on pp. 46-50.

In a footnote to the poem here printed, the editor says : " The reader of taste will easily discover that these stanzas are an early production of our Author's. This is obvious to the editor from the handwriting in the MS. now before him."]

HAIL, ROBIN, blest wi' ilka gift
To spread your fame aneath the lift !
Lang may your Lassie keep in tift
    To rant an' sing,
An' mak thy bonny ballads swift
    O'er Scotia ring.

Poems and Songs, by the late Richard Gall. With a Memoir of the Author. Edinburgh : Oliver and Boyd, MDCCCXIX. 12°.

Whan FERGUSSON (whase blythsome horn
Beguiled the waes he lang had borne)
Frae Caledonia's arms was torn,
    In youthfu' pride,
Unsparing Death deep fixed his thorn
    In Scotia's side.

For, wi' the youth, oh, sad to tell !
Her wonted glee an' spirit fell ;
In ilka howm an' flowery dell
    Mirth fled awa ;
Her pipe hung silent as the shell
    In FINGAL's ha.'

Yet though baith cauld an' laigh he's laid,
Blest ever be his gentle shade !
Since Taste a lightsome charm has spread
    O'er ilka measure,
By auld an' young he'll aye be read
    Wi' waefu' pleasure.

But whan dowf Scotia sighed in pain
For ROBIN's fate—for ROBIN gane—
APOLLO fired a hamely swain
    Wi' mirth an' glee,
An' BURNS revived the joyfu' strain,
    In tunefu' key.

The Scotian Muse, nae langer seen
Wi' bluthered cheeks an' watery een,
Wad lead you through the woodlands green,
    Frae out the thrang,
Wi' her upo' the knowe to lean,
    An' souf a sang.

Fast spreading like a bleezing flame,
The haughs an' vallies rang your fame ;
O'er glens an' braes its echoes came,
  Baith far an' near :
You justly gained a deathless name,
  Beyond compeer.

Your sangs are sought by grit an' sma',
Frae cotter's hut to lordly ha' ;
The Doric pipe sae saft you blaw,
  Wi' breath an' skill.
As gars auld Scotia crously craw
  On ilka hill.

Fu' aft on bonny simmer days,
Whan FLORA wears her gaudy claise,
I dander to the gowany braes,
  Or lanely glens,
To con thy saftly-melting lays,
  Or pawky strains.

O how delightfu' then to lie,
Nor tent the hour that's stealing by,
Till aft you gar me heave a sigh
  'Twixt joy an' grief,
Till ance anither tune you try,
  That brings relief !

Baith fools an' knaves you crously bang,
An' wightly wag the skelping whang,
In words sae pithy, sharp, an' strang,
  An' nicely jointed ;—
Lord pity him wha tholes the stang,
  Sae glegly pointed !

Though little worth your pains I gie,
It's nae for want o' will in me ;
Yet could I think my sangs to thee
        Wad pleasure bring,
Gosh, man ! I'd gladly sit the lee—
        Lang day, an' sing.

Now, wale o' hearty cocks, I feel
I e'en, though laith, maun say, Fareweel ;
For Time, in spite o' ane, will steal
        An' slip awa :
Meanwhile, that I'm your servant leal,
        I'm blythe to shaw.

ADDRESS BY DAVID SILLAR.

[David Sillar, the early friend and corres-
pondent of Burns, was the son of Patrick Sillar,
farmer at Spittleside, near Tarbolton, and was
born there in 1760.   His education, as described
by himself in one of his poems, was limited :

" I ne'er depended for my knowledge
  On school, academy, nor college,
  I gat my learnin' at the flail,
  An' some I catch'd at the plough-tail,
  Amang the brutes I own I'm bred,
  Since herding was my native trade."

Nevertheless he prepared himself for the duties
of a schoolmaster, but was not very successful
in that occupation.   Through his poetical
effusions he made the acquaintance of Burns,
probably about the year 1780, and in May of
the following year was admitted a member of the
Bachelor's Club.   The death of his two brothers,
who had amassed considerable wealth in business,
placed him in comfortable circumstances.   He
was one of the founders of the Irvine Burns'
Club, and was vice-chairman at the first dinner
on the 25th January, 1827.   He was also a
member of the Irvine Town Council and filled
the office of magistrate for two years.   He died
at Irvine on the 2nd of May, 1830.   His
" Poems " were published in an octavo volume
by John Wilson, Kilmarnock, in 1789.]

WHILE Reekie's bards your muse commen',
An' praise the numbers o' your pen,
Accept this kin'ly frae a frien',
    Your Dainty Davie.
Wha ace o' heart does still remain,
    Ye may believe me.

I ne'er was muckle gi'en to praisin',
Or else ye might be sure o' fraisin' :
For trouth, I think, in solid reason,
    Your kintra reed
Plays sweet as Robin Fergusson,
    Or his on Tweed.*

Your *Luath, Caesar* bites right sair ;
An' when ye paint the *Holy Fair*
Ye draw it to a very hair ;
    Or when ye turn,
An' sing the follies o' the Fair,
    How sweet ye mourn !

Let *Coila's* plains wi' me rejoice,
An' praise the worthy *Bard* whose lays,
Their worth and beauty high doth raise
    To lasting fame ;
His works, his worth, will ever praise
    An' crown his name.

Brave Ramsay now an' Fergusson,
Wha hae sae lang time fill'd the Throne
O' Poetry, may now lie down
    Quiet i' their urns,
Since fame, in justice, gies the crown
    To Coila's Burns.

    *Ramsay.

Hail, Happy Bard ! ye're now confest
The king o' singers i' the west :
Edina hath the same exprest ;
     Wi' joy they fin'
That ye're, when tried by Nature's test,
     Gude sterlin' coin.

Sing on my frien', your fame's secured,
An' still maintain the name o' Bard ;
But yet tak' tent an' keep a guard,
     For Envy's tryin'
To blast your name ; mair just reward
     For the envyin'.

But tho' the tout o' Fame may please you,
Let na the flatterin' ghaist o'erheeze you ;
Ne'er flyte nor fraise tae gar fo'k roose you,
     For men o' skill.
When ye write weel, will always praise you
     Out o' gude will.

Great numbers on this earthly ba',
As soon as death gies them the ca',
Permitted are to slide awa',
     An' straught forgot—
Forbid that ever this should fa'
     To be your lot.

I ever had an anxious wish,
Forgive me, Heaven ! if 'twas amiss,
That Fame in life my name would bless,
     An' kin'ly save
It from the cruel tyrant's crush,
     Beyond the grave.

Tho' the fastest liver soonest dies,
An' length o' days sud mak' ane wise ;
Yet haste wi' speed, to glory rise,
    An' spur your horse ;
They're shortest aye wha gain the prize
    Upo' the course.

Sae to conclude, auld frien' an' neebor,
Your muse forgetna weel to feed her,
Then steer through life wi' birr an' vigour
    To win a horn,
Whase soun' shall reach ayont the Tiber
    'Mang ears unborn.

THE GUIDWIFE OF WAUKHOPE HOUSE. TO ROBERT BURNS, THE AYRSHIRE BARD.

February, 1787.

[Elizabeth Scot, "The Guidwife of Wauchope House," was the daughter of David Rutherford of Hermiston Hall, and was born in Edinburgh in 1729. She was thus a niece of Alison or Alicia Rutherford, the authoress of "The Flowers of the Forest," who became in 1731 the wife of Patrick Cockburn of Ormiston. Miss Rutherford received an excellent education, acquiring both Latin and French, and " became a ready proficient in many branches of the belles lettres." She early tried her hand at versification, and one of her pieces, " Solitude and Sadness," greatly charmed Dr. Blacklock. Somewhat late in life she married Walter Scot of Wauchope House, Roxburghshire. In 1801 appeared, posthumously, her " Alonzo and Cora ; to which are added letters in verse by Blacklock and Burns." It is a thin volume, published in London, and edited by someone (evidently a Scot) who preferred to remain anonymous. Most of the verse in the volume is the usual eighteenth century romantic stuff differing little from thousands of other like effusions. The piece which gives title to the volume is taken from Marmontel's " Incas of Peru." The three

F

Scots poems, including the Address to Burns, are the best in the volume, and one cannot but regret that the authoress did not make greater use of her native Doric in her poetical compositions.]

My canty, witty, rhyming ploughman,
I hafflins doubt it is na true, man,
That ye between the stilts was bred,
Wi' ploughmen schooled, wi' ploughmen fed.
I doubt it sair, ye've drawn your knowledge
Either frae grammar-school or college.
Guid troth, your saul and body baith
War better fed, I'd gie my aith,
Than theirs who sup sour milk and parritch,
An' bummil through the single Caritch.
Whaever heard the ploughman speak,
Could tell gif Homer was a Greek ?
He'd flee as soon upon a cudgel,
As get a single line of Virgil.
An' then sae slee ye crack your jokes
O' Willie Pitt and Charlie Fox.
Our great men a' sae weel descrive,
An' how to gar the nation thrive,
Ane maist wad swear ye dwalt amang them,
An' as ye saw them, sae ye sang them.
But be ye ploughmen, be ye peer,
Ye are a funny blade, I swear ;
An' tho' the cauld I ill do bide,
Yet twenty miles, an' mair, I'd ride
O'er moss an' muir, an' never grumble,
Tho' my auld yad should gie a stumble,
To crack a winter-night wi' thee,
An' hear thy sangs and sonnets slee.

A guide saut herring an' a cake,
Wi' sic a cheel a feast wad make,
I'd rather scour your rumming yill,
Or eat o' cheese an' bread my fill,
Than wi' dull lairds on turtle dine,
An' farlie at their wit and wine.
O' gif I kenn'd but whare ye baide,
I'd send to you a marled plaid ;
'Twad haud your shoulders warm and braw,
An' douce at kirk or market shaw ;
Far south, as weel as north, my lad,
A' honest Scotsmen loe the 'maud' ;
Right wae that we're sae far frae ither ;
Yet proud I am to ca' ye brither.

                    Your most obed., E. S.

RHYMING EPISTLE TO MR. R—— B——, AYRSHIRE.

By JAMES MACAULAY.

[James Macaulay was a printer in Edinburgh, and a friend of James Johnson, publisher
of the *Scots Musical Museum*. His Epistle
appeared in his " Poems on various Subjects,
in Scots and English," published in Edinburgh
in 1788. It first appeared in the *Edinburgh
Evening Courant*, June 23, 1787, and was shortly
afterwards reprinted in *The British Chronicle or
Union Gazette*, published in Kelso.]

Weel, *Rab*, I read thestreen your buik,
Frae end to end, an' ne'er forsook
The canty rhimes, till I cou'd brook
          To pore nae mair ;
For Sleep, the weary wight, o'ertook
          An' vex'd me sair.

I never like to mak a fraise,
Or yet be lovich o' my praise,
But I'd maist gi'e my duds o' clae's,
          Gin I cou'd spare them,
Cou'd I but warble furth sic lays,
          An' like you, skair them :

For rich an' poor, an' kirk, an' state,
By turns partake your love an' hate ;
An' mony times you are no blate
          To curse an' bann,
An' speak obscene (ill miss your pate !)
          That's no' the plan.

But whan you crack about the Nine,
An' how to you they've been sae kin',
By helping you the—day to shine
  'Mang Scottish Worthies,
Than you work up a tale fu' fine—
  Wi' weel wal'd wordies.

But still for a' the blast that's made,
I doubt you are some sleekit blade,
That never handled shool or spade,
  Or yet the pleugh,
Unless it were to hae it said—
  An' that's enough :

For by the scraps o' French an' Latin,
That's flung athort your buik fu' thick in,
It's easy seen you've aft been flitting
  Frae school to school ;
An' nae thanks to your head an' wittin',
  Tho' you're nae fool.

I'm no for riving aff your brow,
The laurel folk may think your due ;
But, gin a while you left the pleu'
  To tend the College,
What need you smoor the thing that's true,
  Wi' a' your knowledge ?

The prints—newspapers an' reviews,
Frae time to time may aft you rouse,
An say you're *Heaven-taught*—your views
  Are clear an' fair,
An' a' your ain, gi'en by THE MUSE
  O'er the Banks o' Ayr.

But, waesuck, that'll no gae down
Wi' ilka chiel about this town
That struts in black, an' eke a gown ;
    Na, na, they canna
Believe that poets fa' aroun'.
    Like flakes o' manna !

In days o' yore, folk aft were fleec'd ;
But miracles lang syne hae ceas'd
Amang the gentry here, at least.
    Wha ne'er can think
A bard direct frae Heav'n can feast,
    An' write, an' *drink*.

In a' thing that's in our possession,
We may discern a due progression,
Whilk forces frae us this confession,
    Man didna fa'.
Down frae the lift without transgression
    Or yet a flaw.

You've surely notic'd this yoursel',
Afore we read, we aye maun spell :
An' till the chucky leave the shell
    Whar it was hidden,
It canna soun' the morning bell
    Upo' your midden.

The grain you t' ither day did saw
Ayont the knowe, was smoor'd wi' snaw,
An' summer suns maun gar it blaw,
    Ere it be ready
For Autumn's sonsy lassies braw
    To mak it teddy.

Ilk thing in Nature has a time,
When ane may say, it's in its prime,
An' disna in a hurry climb
      To real perfection.
But maun gae thro' its ilka clime,
      An' ain direction.

It's just the same, (for ought I ken),
Amang the folk that lifts the pen,
To write on kingdoms, brutes, or men ;
      Ane's brains sae stappit,
Mony a owk on lear we spen',
      To clear our *caput.*

This being than a settled case,
Ne'er try to put things out o' place ;
But own your intellects you brace
      Wi' solid lore,
As mony a ane, wi' honest face,
      Has done afore.

EPISTLE FROM THOMAS WALKER.

[Thomas Walker, a tailor living near Ochiltree, was an intimate friend of William Simson, the schoolmaster, to whom Burns addressed his poetical epistle, " I gat your letter, winsome Willie." " Walker, like Simson, could write verses. Seeing how successful his friend had been in ' drawing ' Burns, he thought to do likewise, and sent the poet a long-winded epistle containing twenty-six stanzas. Burns took no notice of it. On the appearance of the Kilmarnock edition, Walker made another attempt to attract the poet's attention, and, by attacking him in the character of a moral censor, succeeded. Burns answered him in the "Reply to an Epistle received from a Tailor " (Wallace-Chambers, v. 1, p. 402). Walker's Epistle originally consisted of twenty-one stanzas, but was cut down to ten by Simson before it was printed by Stewart in the volume of " Poems ascribed to Robert Burns, the Ayrshire Bard," published in Glasgow in 1801.]

WHAT waefu' news is this I hear,
Frae greeting I can scarce forbear,
Folks tell me ye' ar gaun aff this year
    Out owre the sea,
And lasses, wham ye lo'e sae dear,
    Will greet for thee.

Weel wad I like war ye to stay,
But, Robin, since ye will away,
I hae a word yet mair to say,
        And maybe twa :
May He protect us night an' day,
        That made us a'.

Whare art thou gaun, keep mind frae me,
Seek Him to bear thee companie,
And, Robin, whan ye come to die,
        Ye'll won aboon,
An' live at peace an' unity
        Ayont the moon.

Some tell me, Rab, ye dinna fear
To get a wean, an' curse an' swear,
I'm unco wae, my lad, to hear
        O' sic a trade ;
Could I persuade ye to forbear,
        I wad be glad.

Fu' weel ye ken ye'll gang to—
Gin ye persist in doing ill—
Waes me ! ye're hurlin' down the hill
        Withouten dread,
An' ye'll get leave to swear your fill
        After ye're dead.

There, walth o' women ye'll get near,
But getting' weans ye will forbear,
Ye'll never say, my bonnie dear
        Come, gie's a kiss—
Nae kissing there—ye'll girn an' sneer,
        An'ither hiss.

O Rab ! lay by thy foolish tricks,
An' steer nae mair the female sex,
Or some day ye'll come through the pricks,
  An' that ye'll see :
Ye'll find hard living wi' Auld Nicks ;
  I'm wae for thee.

But what's this comes wi' sic a knell,
Amaist as loud as ony bell,
While it does mak' my conscience tell
  Me what is true,
I'm but a ragget cowt mysel',
  Owre sib to you !

We're owre like those wha think it fit
To stuff their noddles fu' o' wit,
An' yet content in darkness sit,
  Wha shun the light,
To let them sae down to the pit,
  That lang dark night.

But fareweel, Rab, I maun awa',
May He that made us keep us a',
For that wad be a dreadfu' fa',
  And hurt us sair ;
Lad, we wad never mend ava,
  Sae, Rab, tak' care.

VERSES BY JANET LITTLE.

[Janet Little, "The Scotch Milkmaid," as
she is described on the title-page of her volume
of poems, was the daughter of George Little in
Nether Bogside, near Ecclefechan, Dumfriesshire,
and was born in the same year as Burns. She
died in 1813. For a girl in her station of life she
acquired a fairly good education, and early
displayed a great love of reading along with a
facility in rhyming. After some years in service
with the Rev. Mr. Johnstone and with Mrs.
Dunlop of Dunlop, she engaged herself with Mrs.
Henri at Loudoun House to take charge of the
dairy—hence her cognomen of "The Scotch
Milkmaid." While in service at Loudoun she
addressed (12th July, 1789) the following poetical
epistle to Burns, to which he probably replied,
though there is no record of his having done so.
From the remark in his letter to Mrs. Dunlop
(6th September, 1789), it would appear that he
did not. In 1792 her poems were published
under the title of "The Poetical Works of Janet
Little, the Scotch Milkmaid," from the press of
John and Peter Wilson of Ayr. Her Epistle to
the Poet occurs on pp. 160-163, and the lines on
her visit to Ellisland on pp. 111-112. In
Blackie's edition of the Works of Burns the
penultimate verse of her Epistle reads as follows :

" Sure Milton's eloquence were faint
   The beauties of your verse to paint ;
My rude unpolish'd strokes but taint
    Their brilliancy ;
     The attempt would doubtless vex a saint,
     And weel may thee."]

FAIR fa' the honest rustic swain,
The pride o' a' our Scottish plain :
Thou gies us joy to hear thy strain,
    And notes sae sweet ;
Old Ramsay's shade reviv'd again,
    In thee we greet.

Lov'd Thallia, that delightful muse,
Seem'd long shut up as a recluse ;
To all she did her aid refuse,
    Since Allan's day.
Till Burns arose, then did she choose
    To grace his lay.

To hear thy sang, all ranks desire ;
Sae weel you strik'st the dormant lyre ;
Apollo, wi' poetic fire,
    Thy breast did warm,
An' critics silently admire
    Thy art to charm.

Cæsar an' Luath weel can speak ;
'Tis pity e'er their gabs should steek,
But into human nature keek,
    An' knots unravel ;
To hear their lectures ance a-week,
    Ten miles I'd travel.

Thy dedication to G—— H——,
In unco bonny, hamespun speech,
Wi' winsome glee the heart can teach
    A better lesson
Than servile bards who fawn an' fleech
    Like beggar's messin.

When slighted love becomes thy theme,
An' woman's faithless vows you blame,
With so much pathos you exclaim,
     In your Lament,
But glanc'd by the most frigid dame,
     She wad relent.

The daisy too, you sing wi' skill ;
An' weel ye praise the whisky gill.
In vain I blunt my feckless quill
     Your fame to raise,
While echo sounds, frae ilka hill,
     To Burns's praise.

Did Addison or Pope but hear
Or Sam, that critic must severe,
A plough-boy sing, with throat sae clear,
     They, in a rage,
Their works wad a' in pieces tear
     An' curse your page.

If I should strain my rupy throat,
To raise thy praise wi' swelling note,
My rude, unpolish'd strokes wad blot
     Thy brilliant shine,
An' ev'ry passage I would quote
     Seem less sublime.

The task I'll drop ; wi' heart sincere
To heav'n present a humble prayer,
That a' the blessings mortals share
     May be, by turns,
Dispens'd with an indulgent care
     To Robert Burns.

ON A VISIT TO MR. BURNS.

JANET LITTLE.

[Sometime in the beginning of 1791 Janet undertook a journey to Dumfriesshire for the double purpose of visiting her relatives and of obtaining an interview with Burns at Ellisland. The Poet was absent on Excise duty when she arrived, but soon after appeared with an arm broken through a fall from his horse. Janet described the scene in the following lines.]

Is 't true ? or does some magic spell
    My wond'ring eyes beguile ?
In this the place where deigns to dwell
    The honour of our isle ?

The charming BURNS, the Muse's care,
    Of all her sons the pride ;
This pleasure oft I've sought to share,
    But been as oft deni'd.

Oft have my thoughts, at midnight hour,
    To him excursions made ;
This bless in dreams was premature,
    And with my slumbers fled.

'Tis real now, no vision here
    Bequeaths a poignant dart ;
I'll view the poet ever dear,
    Whose lays have charm'd my heart.

Hark ! now he comes, a dire alarm
   Re-echoes through his hall !
Pegasus* kneel'd, his rider's arm
   Was broken by a fall.

The doleful tidings to my ears
   Were in harsh notes convey'd ;
His lovely wife stood drown'd in tears,
   While thus I pond'ring said :

" No cheering draught, with ills unmix'd,
   Can mortals taste below ;
All human fate by heav'n is fix'd,
   Alternate joy and wo."

With beating breast I view'd the bard ;
   All trembling did him greet ;
With sighs bewail'd his fate so hard,
   Whose notes were ever sweet.

*The name of the Poet's horse.

EPISTLES FROM THOMAS TELFORD.

[Thomas Telford, the celebrated engineer, was born in Eskdale, Dumfriesshire, in 1757, and died in London in 1834. He received but a limited education in the parish school of Westerkirk, but afterwards taught himself the Latin, German, French and Italian languages. Apprenticed as a mason in his fourteenth year he amused himself by contributing several poetical pieces to *Ruddiman's Weekly Magazine*, an Edinburgh periodical, under the signature of " Eskdale Tam." Shortly after the publication of Burns's volume in 1786 he addressed an epistle in rhyme to the poet, the following portion of which is printed in Currie's edition of the Works of Burns. (v. 1, Appendix No. 2). The poem as a whole does not appear ever to have been printed. Currie prefaces the stanzas with the following words : " A great number of manuscript poems were found among the papers of Burns, addressed to him by admirers of his genius, from different parts of Britain, as well as from Ireland and America. Among these was a poetical epistle from Mr. Telford, of superior merit. It is written in the dialect of Scotland . . . . and in the versification generally employed by our poet himself. Its object is to recommend to him other subjects of a serious nature, similar to that of the *Cottar's Saturday Night;* and the reader will find that the advice is happily enforced by

example. It would have given the editor
pleasure to have inserted the whole of this poem,
which he hopes will one day see the light : he is
happy to have obtained, in the meantime, his
friend Mr. Telford's permission to insert the
following extracts."]

*   *   *   *   *

Pursue, O Burns ! thy happy style,
" Those manner-painting strains," that while
They bear me northward mony a mile,
        Recall the days,
When tender joys, with pleasing smile.
        Blest my young ways.

I see my fond companions rise,
I join the happy village joys,
I see our green hills touch the skies,
        And thro' the woods,
I hear the river's rushing noise,
        Its roaring floods.*

No distant Swiss with warmer glow,
E'er heard his native music flow,
Nor could his wishes stronger grow,
        Than still have mine,
When up this ancient mount I go,†
        With songs of thine.

---

*The banks of the *Esk* in Dumfriesshire are here alluded to.

†A beautiful little mount, which stands immediately before, or
   rather forms a part of Shrewsbury Castle, a seat of Sir
   William Pulteney, Bart.

O happy Bard ! thy gen'rous flame,
Was given to raise thy country's fame,
For this thy charming numbers came,
    Thy matchless lays ;
Then sing, and save her virtuous name,
    To latest days.

    *   *   *   *   *

But mony a theme awaits thy muse,
Fine as thy Cotter's sacred views,
Then in such verse thy soul infuse,
    With holy air,
And sing the course the pious chuse,
    With all thy care.

How with religious awe imprest,
They open lay the guileless breast,
And youth and age with fears distrest,
    All due prepare,
The symbols of eternal rest
    Devout to share.*

How down ilk lang withdrawing hill,
Successive crowds the valleys fill,
While pure religious converse still
    Beguile the way,
And gives a cast to youthful will,
    To suit the day.

*The Sacrament, generally administered in the country parishes of
  Scotland in the open-air.

How plac'd along the sacred board,
Their hoary pastor's looks ador'd,
His voice with peace and blessings stor'd,
        Sent from above,
And faith, and hope, and joy afford,
        And boundless love.

O'er this with warm seraphic glow,
Celestial beings pleased bow,
And, whisper'd, hear the holy vow,
        'Mid grateful tears ;
And mark amid such scenes below,
        Their future peers.

*   *   *   *   *

O mark the awful, solemn scene !*
When hoary winter clothes the plain,
Along the snowy hills is seen
        Approaching slow,
In mourning weeds, the village train,
        In silent woe.

Some much-respected brother's bier,
(By turns in pious task they share),
With heavy hearts they forward bear
        Along the path ;
Where nei'bours saw, in dusky air,†
        The light of death.

*A Scottish funeral.

†This alludes to a superstition prevalent in Eskdale and
    Annandale, that a light precedes in the night every funeral,
    marking the precise path it is to pass.

And when they pass the rocky how,
Where binwood bushes o'er them flow,
And move around the rising knowe,
  Where far away
The kirk yard trees are seen to grow,
  By th' water brae.

Assembled round the narrow grave,
While o'er them wintry tempests rave,
In the cold wind their grey locks wave,
  As low they lay
Their brother's body 'mongst the lave
  Of parent clay.

Expressive looks from each declare
The griefs within their bosoms bear,
One holy bow devout they share,
  Then home return,
And think o'er all the virtues fair
  Of him they mourn.

  * * * * *

Say how by early lessons taught,
(Truth's pleasing air is willing caught),
Congenial to th' untainted thought,
  The shepherd boy,
Who tends his flocks on lonely height,
  Feels holy joy.

Is aught on earth so lovely known,
On Sabbath morn and far alone,
His guileless soul all naked shown
  Before his God—
Such pray'rs must welcome reach the throne,
  And blest abode.

O tell ! with what a heartfelt joy,
The parent eyes the virtuous boy ;
And all his constant kind employ,
    Is how to give
The best of lear he can enjoy,
    As means to live.

The parish school, its curious site,
The master who can clear indite,
And lead him on to count and write,
    Demand thy care ;
Nor pass the ploughman's school at night
    Without a share.

Nor yet the tenty curious lad
Who o'er the ingle hings his head,
And begs of nei'bours books to read ;
    For hence arise
Thy country's sons, who far are spread,
    Baith bauld and wise.

*   *   *   *   *

The bonny lasses, as they spin,
Perhaps with Allan's sangs begin,
How Tay and Tweed smooth flowing rin
    Thro' flowery hows ;
Where shepherd lads their sweethearts win
    With earnest vows.

Or may be, Burns, thy thrilling page
May a' their virtuous thoughts engage,
While playful youth and placid age
    In concert join,
To bless the bard, who, gay or sage,
    Improves the mind.

Long may their harmless simple ways,
Nature's own pure emotions raise ;
May still the dear romantic blaze
    Of purest love,
Their bosoms warm to latest days,
    And aye improve.

May still each fond attachment glow,
O'er woods, o'er streams, o'er hills of snow ;
May rugged rocks still dearer grow,
    And may their souls
Even love the warlock glens which through
    The tempest howls.

To eternize such themes as these,
And all their happy manners seize,
Will ever virtuous bosom please,
    And high in fame
To future times will justly raise
    Thy patriot name.

While all the venal tribes decay,
That bask in flatt'ry's flaunting ray,
The noisome vermin of a day,
    Thy works shall gain
O'er every mind a boundless sway,
    And lasting reign.

When winter binds the harden'd plains,
Around each hearth, the hoary swains,
Shall teach the rising youth thy strains,
    And anxious say
Our blessing with our sons remains,
    And BURNS'S LAY !

LETTERS FROM DR. BLACKLOCK TO THE POET

[Dr. Thomas Blacklock, author of the two following poetical letters, was born of humble parentage at Annan in 1721, and died in Edinburgh in 1791. He lost his sight through smallpox when about six months old. In boyhood he was educated by having people read to him, and afterwards completed his education at the University of Edinburgh. He was ordained minister of Kirkcudbright in 1762, but the congregation objected to his appointment by reason of his infirmity. In 1764 he resigned the charge and removed to Edinburgh. It was his letter to Dr. Laurie, the minister of Loudoun, expressing high appreciation of Burns's volume that caused the Poet to alter his resolution about going to the West Indies, and "thus, to all human appearance, saved from oblivion the greatest lyrist that the world has seen."]

To Mr. ROBERT BURNS

EDINBURGH, *24th August*, 1789

DEAR BURNS, thou brother of my heart,
Both for thy virtues and thy art ;
If art it may be called in thee,
Which Nature's bounty large and free
With pleasure in thy breast diffuses,
And warms thy soul with all the Muses.
Whether to laugh with easy grace
Thy numbers move the sage's face,

Or bid the softer passions rise,
And ruthless souls with grief surprise,
'Tis Nature's voice distinctly felt
Through thee, her organ, thus to melt.

Most anxiously I wish to know,
With thee of late how matters go ;
How keeps of late thy much-loved Jean her health ?
What promises thy farm of wealth ?
Whether the Muse persists to smile,
And all thy anxious cares beguile ?
Whether bright fancy keeps alive ?
And how thy darling infants thrive ?

For me, with grief and sickness spent,
Since I my homeward journey bent,
Spirits depressed no more I mourn,
But vigour, life and health return.
No more to gloomy thoughts a prey,
I sleep all night and live all day ;
By turns my friend and book enjoy,
And thus my circling hours employ ;
Happy while yet these hours remain,
I Burns could join the cheerful train,
With wounted zeal, sincere and fervent
Salute once more his humble servant,

                    THOMAS BLACKLOCK.

[In September, 1790, Dr. Blacklock
addressed the following playful poetical epistle
to Burns along with a prospectus of a new
periodical to be called *The Bee*. In the letter he
introduces Dr. James Anderson (1739-1808),
the editor, to the Poet's notice and entreats him
to become an occasional contributor to the
periodical.]

EDINBURGH, 1790.

How does my dear friend (much I languish to hear),
His fortune, relations, and all that are dear ?
With love of the Muses so strongly still smitten,
I meant this epistle in verse to have written ;
But from age and infirmity, indolence flows,
And this, much I fear, will restore me to prose.
Anon to my business I wish to proceed,—
Dr. Anderson guides and provokes me to speed,
A man of integrity, genius and worth,
Who soon a performance intends to set forth ;
A work miscellaneous, extensive and free
Which will weekly appear, by the name of *The Bee*,
Of this from himself I inclose you a plan,
And hope you will give what assistance you can.
Entangled with business, and haunted with care
In which more or less human nature must share,
Some moments of leisure the Muses will claim,
A sacrifice due to amusement and fame,
The Bee which sucks honey from every gay bloom,
With some rays of your genius her work may illume,
Whilst the flower whence her honey spontaneously flows
As fragrantly smells and as vig'rously grows.
Now with kind gratulations 'tis time to conclude,
And add, your promotion is here understood ;
Thus free from the servile employ of excise, Sir,
We hope soon to hear you commence supervisor,
You then, more at leisure, and free from control,
May indulge the strong passion that reigns in your soul ;
But I, feeble I, must to nature give way,
Devoted cold death's and longevity's pray,
From verses though languid my thoughts must unbend,
Tho' still I remain your affectionate friend,

THOMAS BLACKLOCK.

SONNET BY MISS HELEN MARIA WILLIAMS ON READING "THE MOUNTAIN DAISY," BY ROBERT BURNS.

[Miss Helen Maria Williams was born in London in 1762, and spent the earlier years of her life at Berwick-on-Tweed. She was introduced to Burns by Dr. Moore, and in June 1787 sent the Poet a letter telling him that, from her mother being a Scotswoman, she understood the language in which his poems were written, and "had read his poems with satisfaction, and shared the triumph of his country in producing his laurels." She also sent the Poet a poem of her own on *The Slave Trade* which Burns (August, 1789) criticised at length in an answer to her. She settled in Paris about 1790, and was imprisoned for a time as a partisan of the Gironde. Her literary work includes a novel, *Julia*, published in 1790, several works on France, a good deal of verse, besides numerous contributions to the poetical and political literature of the period. She died in Paris in December, 1827.]

WHILE soon " the garden's flaunting flowers " decay,
    And scatter'd on the earth neglected lie,
The " Mountain Daisy," cherish'd by the ray
    A poet drew from heav'n, shall never die.

Ah, like that lovely flower the poet rose !
    'Mid penury's bare soil and bitter gale ;
He felt each storm that on the mountain blows,
    Nor ever knew the shelter of the vale.

By genius in her native vigor nurst,
  On nature with impassion'd look he gazed ;
Then through the cloud of adverse fortune burst
  Indignant, and in light unborrow'd blazed.

Scotia ! from rude affliction shield thy bard
His heav'n-taught numbers fame herself will guard.

THE BARD : A POEM IN THE MANNER OF SPENSER.

INSCRIBED TO MR. R—— B——.

[Gavin Turnbull, the author of this Epistle, is believed to have been born in Hawick, Roxburghshire, in 1758. When a lad his parents removed to Kilmarnock, where he received a fairly good education. Family misfortunes blighted his future prospects, and, like Ebenezer Picken, he had a hard struggle through life. Bred to carpet-weaving he eventually became an actor. He made the acquaintance of Burns in 1786, and when a member of Sutherland's company renewed his acquaintance with the Poet in Dumfries in 1793. Burns sent some of his songs to George Thomson, for publication in the *Melodies*, and evidently thought well of his productions. Turnbull afterwards emigrated to America in 1792, "and the remainder of his history is a blank." His *Poetical Essays* were published in Glasgow by David Niven in 1788, and a second edition appeared in 1794.*]

Dear to the Muse, who gave his days to flow,
With mighty blessings, mix'd with mighty wo.

Pope's Homer.

---

*The archaisms in this poem are explained at the end of the Scottish glossary.

I.

Happy the youth, on whom dame fortune smiles,
And gives him wealth, his wishes to pursue ;
The jocund hours he easily beguiles,
Still steering on to pleasures ever new.
And if fair Science can attract his view,
Enamour'd of the worthy Bards of old,
He knows not the distresses of the crew,
On whom the beldam ne'er her favours roll'd,
Or him whose hapless fate I purpose to unfold.

II.

O thou, who from the pleasant banks of Ayr
Thy merit summon'd to Edina's walls,
Whose songs delight her sons and daughters fair,
And loudly echo through her splendid halls.
On thee a simple Poet humbly calls,
A simple Poet who obscur'd the while,
The fear of scornful critic sore appals,
On whom, if Coila's Bard vouchsafe to smile,
His name shall spread abroad thro' Albion's sea-girt Isle

III.

There whilom ligd, ypent in garret high,
A tuneful Bard, who well could touch the lyre,
Who often sung to soot, and witchingly
As made the crowds, in silent gaze, admire,
Ymolten with the wild seraphic fire
Which his sweet sonnets eathly could impart,
They list'ning stood, ne never did they tire,
So steal'd his soft persuasion on the heart,
So smooth his numbers flow'd, all unrestrain'd by art.

IV.

Sometimes, as fancy prompt him, he would sing,
The charms of nature at the morning's dawn,
Or paint the beauties of the blooming spring,
The shady forest, and the flow'ry lawn,
The whitened thorn and roses newly blawn,
Or mazy rills, that wildly devious flow,
Or pensive shepherd, from the crowd withdrawn,
Sore pin'd with luckless love and mochel wo,
Design'd from tow'ring cliff his wretched self to throw.

V.

Eftsoons he changed quite the veering strain,
To winter shrouded in her mantle hoar,
The boreal blast, the bitter driving rain,
The swelling torrents loud resounding roar,
Which down the steep, the groaning forest bore,
And delug'd all the swimming plains below ;
Then snug the lake with ice ycover'd o'er,
The nimble youngsters, hurling to and fro,
And mountain's heaving head yclad in virgin snow.

VI.

" Now shut the pond'rous gate, and rouse the fire,
Produce the flask, and fill the massy bowl ;
To gloomy haunt let wrinkl'd care retire,
Let joy abound possessing ev'ry soul,
Let Boreas bluster, and the tempest howl ;
'Tis ours to snatch the pleasures, as they fly,
Now up the lofty Diapason rowl,
'Tis music gives the purest extacy,
And lifts the soul from earth exalted to the sky.

VII.

" See where the miser, brooding o'er his gear,
Sits sad and sullen, in his dreary cell,
No glowing fire, the sable walls to cheer,
With him pale want and timid fancy dwell.
O ! tell us true, ye wretched miscreants tell,
Why all this caution to secure your gold,
Will it appease the ruthless King of hell,
Or help to make the burning climate cold,
Ah ! vain your hope, for there no joy is bought or sold.

VIII.

" Let the dull Cynic preach his musty rules,
No son of Bacchus will attend his lore ;
Let him hold forth to children and to fools,
And turn, and turn his lifeless lectures o'er ;
And cite old Plato, and ilk sage of yore,
And beat his breast, and grin and look awry,
Down with the pedant, let us sing and roar :
Behold the festive moments dancing by,
'Tis ours in joy to live, and catch them as they fly."

IX.

Thus flow'd his numbers, to the jolly train,
While buoyant spirits kept his soul above,
Then grief would interfere, and damp his strain,
And gloomy thoughts and sad ideas move ;
Then like a weary wight enthrall'd in love,
Of flames and chains, and arrows would he tell,
And, sadly sighing, seek the gloomy grove,
Or ruin, seated in a dreary dell,
Whence oft, at dead of night, grim ghosts terrific yell.

X.

What'er he sung, or pleasing or sublime,
The placid verses always run the same ;
Did love or friendship e'er demand his rhyme,
Or wight grotesque his meditation claim,
With equal force and energy they came,
And pity or loud laughter could ymove,
So eath he trode the arduous path of fame
And so engross'd the tuneful sisters' love,
None rival could his lays, so far less reach above.

XI.

Now Fame, with brazen tromp, proclaimed loud
His name, which through all Caledonia rung,
The busy murmur spread along the crowd,
In ev'ry place, his roundelays are sung,
Improven much, by ev'ry female tongue,
To whom the songs of love are ever dear,
The grave, the gay, the am'rous and the young,
All crowd around the wondrous Bard to hear,
For ne'er did Scottish Bard so much enchant the ear.

XII.

But, will the sweet delusion ever last ?
Will ay his reputation firm remain ?
Ah me ! I fear misfortune's ruthless blast,
That still o'ertakes the muses' gentle train,
Expos'd to poverty, and cold disdain
Of witless louts, who see them passen by,
And eke the beau, of gaudy trappings vain,
Who on their tatter'd vestments cast an eye,
Gods ! what a silly soul, the witless creatures cry.

XIII.

She next display'd before his wondering eyes,
A laurel crown, and thus her speech begun,
" The youth who hopes to gain the mighty prize,
The busy ways of avarice must shun,
And from the haunts of low ambition run,
Accurs'd is he who sings for worthless ore,
Such of Apollo never favour won ;
The most illustrious of the Bards of yore,
Pale poverty, and want, and mighty sorrows bore."

XIV.

Admonish'd thus, he never crept abroad,
Nor long'd to mingle in the busy coil,
Though others idoliz'd the Aureat God,
Ne never longs to share the filthy spoil,
Ne fit for hurry, and disdaining toil,
Assiduously, he turns the classic page,
Which treats of war and many a bloody broil,
How rival God's Ilium's cause engage,
And seems inspir'd with all Dan Homer's Epic rage.

XV.

How good Æneas from the fatal shore,
Convey'd his household Gods and aged Sire,
The mournful fate of murder'd Polydore,
Poor Dido flaming on the funeral pire,
When she beheld the Trojan fleet retire ;
The Cumæan oracle, the branch of gold,
The reign of Pluto, and his mansion dire,
What wondrous things Anchises did unfold,
And all that e'er the charming Bard of Mantua told.

H

XVI.

Sometimes the past'ral numbers he would read,
Where is depainted many a simple swain,
Supinely piping on the flow'ry mead,
Sicilian valley or Arcadian plain.
Where pass their golden days withouten pain :
Or trace the am'rous Ovid's witching lay,
Or smooth Tibullus' soft pathetic strain,
Sharp Juvenal, and Horace ever gay,
Bards who the utmost pow'r of human wit display.

XVII.

On wooden shelves were fav'rite authors plac'd,
Gilt on the backs, and rang'd in seemly row ;
The Bard and sage, his ample study grac'd,
Historians wise, and many authors moe ;
There painted maps enhanc'd the learned show,
Where all the word in miniature was seen,
The landscape did with gaudy colours glow,
The airy mountain, and the forest green,
Which all yblent produc'd goodly scene I ween.

XVIII.

The floor with scrolls of paper was besprent,
And musty pamphlets, which disorder'd lay,
An Epic Poem, here in pieces rent,
And there appear'd the fragments of a Play,
Which was to be revis'd some other day,
And gain a crowded Theatre's applause ;
And here an Ode a mouse had stolen away,
A mouse as learn'd as Shenstone's rottan was,*
But thoughtlessly enthrall'd in fell grimalkin's claws.

*See the rape of the trap.

XIX.

Now would he quickly take a volume down,
And read, with face demure a page or twain,
Catch at a hint, and mark it for his own,
And place his benefactor right again,
Then, with the thought, the marble paper stain,
And gaze upon it, with enraptur'd look,
Ay walking to and fro, nae little vain ;
Encourag'd thus, he reassumes the book,
To seek for more from whence the other hint he took.

XX.

Thus spent he many a long and dreary day,
With lean repast, not over merrily,
For all unkempt he never lov'd to stray,
Save when the gleaming moon illum'd the sky,
When none his tatter'd liv'ry mote espy ;
Then would he stolen softly from his dome,
And to some haunted stream 's meanders hy,
And sullen, stalking through the solemn gloom,
Some sadly plaintive strain or Elegy resume.

XXI.

But O ! what pen his terror can describe,
When to his lofty mansion slow ascends,
A Caitiff, dreadful to the tuneful tribe,
Yclep'd a dun, a catchpoll him attends,
And in his fist a magic wand extends,
Thund'ring they bawl, he trembles at the roar,
His breath he stifles, and his voice suspends,
And lies entranc'd, like Mahomet of yore,
Ne offers he to stir till after the siege is o'er.

XXII.

So crafty Reynard, that nocturnal pest,
Descends, in silence, from the cloudy hill ;
When all the village curs and mastiffs rest,
The roost to pillage, and the geese to kill,
Which having done, and eat and drunk his fill,
Prepar'd for flight, the trap blockades the way,
The farmer comes, and finds him lying still,
Stretch'd on the ground, a lump of breathless clay,
But soon as he is gone, the villain sneaks away.

LINES ON BURNS.

By HENRY ADDINGTON, VISCOUNT SIDMOUTH.

[Henry Addington, Viscount Sidmouth, was born in London in 1757, the son of Lord Chatham's physician, Dr. Anthony Addington. After completing his studies at Brasenose College, Oxford, in 1778, he studied law, but his friendship with Pitt led him to adopt a political career. He was created Viscount Sidmouth in 1805, was thrice President of the Council, once Lord Privy Seal, and for nine years held the office of Home Secretary. He died in 1844. Allan Cunningham states that the Duchess of Gordon, knowing that he was a warm admirer of Burns's poetry, "planned a meeting between them, with Dr. Beattie, at Gordon Castle. The future premier," says Cunningham, "was unable to accept the invitation; but wrote and forwarded, it is said, these memorable lines— memorable as the first indication of that deep love which England now entertains for the genius of Burns."]

YES! pride of Scotia's favoured plains, 'tis thine
  The warmest feelings of the heart to move ;
To bid it throb with sympathy divine,
  To glow with friendship or to melt with love.

What though each morning sees thee rise to toil,
  Though Plenty on thy cot no blessing showers,
Yet independence cheers thee with her smile,
  And Fancy strews thy moorland with her flowers !

And dost thou blame the impartial will of Heaven,
  Untaught of life the good and ill to scan ?
To thee the Muse's choicest wreath is given—
  To thee the genuine dignity of man !

Then, to the want of wordly gear resigned,
Be grateful for the wealth of thy exhaustless mind.

GLOSSARY

A', all.
Abee, alone.
Ablins, aiblins, perhaps, possibly.
Ae, a.
Aff, off.
Aft, oft, often.
Aiblins. See *ablins*.
Ain, own.
Aith, oath.
Aiver, old horse.
Allevoly, giddy, frivolous.
Ance, once.
Are n'ye, are you not.
Arrils, one's deserts.
A's, all is.
Attour, over.
Aul', old, aged.
Auld Cloots, the Devil.
Auld-farran, aulfarrant, old-fashioned
Ava, at all.
Ayont, beyond.

Baide, dwelt, resided.
Bairnies, children.
Baith, both.
Ban, abuse (verbally).
Bannin', cursing.
Bannock, oatmeal cake.
Barrow, borrow.
Baul', bauld, bold.
Baun, band.
Bawbee, old Scots coin, a half-penny.
Begoud, began.
Beil, beild, biel, bield, shelter.
Ben, in, within.
Bend the bicker, drink off the bicker or glass, applied to one who drinks immoderately.
Beuk, biuk, buik, book.
Beukie, dimin. of *beuk*, booklet.
Bicker, repeatedly attack.
Biel, bield. See under *beil*.
Binwood, ivy.
Birkie, lively smart young fellow.

Bit, but.
Bizz, buzz, bustle.
Bla', blow.
Blate, bashful, timid.
Bleaz'd, blazed.
Bleezing, blazing.
Blether, n. idle talk; v. talk idly.
Blin', blind.
Bluid, blood.
Blun'er, blundering, stupidity.
Bluthered cheeks, cheeks wet and stained with tears.
Bombaze, confound.
Bonnie, bonny, bony, beautiful, handsome, attractive.
Boon a', above all.
Boost, behooved.
Boot, behooved.
Bot, without.
Bra', braw, excellent, handsome.
Brag, challenge.
Braid, broad.
Brawly, well, intimately.
Brecham, collar of a working horse.
Breekless, trouser-less, *i.e.*, kilted.
Breeks, trousers.
Breuk, broke.
Brigs, bridges.
Brocket phiz, sooty faced.
Broo, brow.
Brook, enjoy.
Brunt, burnt, burned.
Buik. See under *beuk*.
Bummil, to read indistinctly.
Burnie, streamlet.
Buskit, dressed.
Byre, cow-house.

Ca', call.
Ca'd, called.
Caff, chaff.
Calked, chalked.
Callan, lad, youth; pl. *callans*.
Canty, lively, cheerful.

Caritch, Catechism; *single Caritch*, the Shorter Catechism.
Carle, man.
Ca't, call it.
Caterans, Highland robbers.
Caukt, chalked, written with chalk.
Cauld, cold.
Chang, musical sound.
Cheek for chow, side by side.
Cheel, chiel, man, companion.
Chill, child.
Chow, See under *cheek*.
Chucky, young chick.
Claes, claise, clothes.
Claise. See under *claes*.
Clatter, to talk familiarly with.
Claw, scratch.
Clishmaclavers, idle talk, false reports.
Cock. See under *hearty*.
Commaun, command.
Coof, fool.
Coost, cast.
Cosh, familiar, friendly.
Coutter, coulter.
Cozie, snug, comfortable.
Crack, converse.
Cracket, cracked, snapped (?)
Cracks, chats, talks.
Craik, croak.
Craw, crow.
Croon, crown, five shillings.
Crouse, cruse, proud.
Crousely, proudly, boldly.
Crune, croon, hum.
Cust the hule, cast off the husk, *i.e.*, was born.
Cuttie-stool, stool of repentance on which offenders formerly sat in church in face of the congregation.

Dab, specialist, expert.
Daffin, loose talk, sport.
Dander, stroll, wander.
Dane, done.
Darna, dare not.
Dee, die.
Deil be licket, nothing at all.
Dight, prepare.

Ding, excel.
Dink, neat, dainty.
Dinna, do not.
Dis, does.
Dis, doest.
Divall, cease.
Doon, done.
Douce, respectable.
Dour, stubborn.
Dow, a term of affection.
Dowf, sad, melancholy.
Dowie, in Skinner's verse "used as denoting the visible effect of age on poetical composition."
Downa, cannot, durst not.
Dredgy, funeral service, "the fuddle after the funeral."
Dried, endured, suffered.
Duddies, clothes, garments.
Duds o' claes,
Dush, dish.

E'e, eye.
Een, eyes.
eild, age.
Eneuch, enough.
Ettle, attempt, aim.
Exquees'd, excused.

Fa', fall.
Fain. See under *unco*.
Fair fa', good luck to; an expression of good wishes.
Fan, when.
Fankit, "fankit i' my tether," *i.e.*, fastened in my stall.
Farlie, n. and v., wonder.
Fash, trouble.
Fasht, troubled.
Fat, what.
Faul', fold.
Faund, found.
Fausely, falsely.
Fau't, fault.
Fawn an' fleech, fawn and flatter.
Feard, afraid.
Feck, part (of the time).
Feckfu', resourceful.
Feckless, feeble.
Feel, fool; adj. foolish.

Fegs, faith. *My fegs*, truly.
Feinzie, feign.
Fidging fain, eager with restlessness.
Fike, worry, vex (themselves).
Fin', find.
Fistling, rustling, whistling.
Flee, fly.
Flee, frighten.
Fleech. See under *fawn*.
Fleeching. flattering.
Fleeps, stupid fellows.
Flirds, vain finery.
Flittin', moving, flitting.
Flyte, v., scold ; n., scolding.
Foggy, mossy.
Fouth, abundance, plenty.
Fouk, fowk, people, folk.
Fozie, feeble.
Frae, from.
Fraise, flatter, cajole.
Fraisin', flattery, cajolery ; v. flattering.
Fremmit, strange, foreign.
Fribble, trifler.
Frichts, frights, frightful beings.
Fu', full.
Fur and rigg, furrow and ridge of a ploughed field.
Furthy, affable.
Fyk'd, troubled, uneasy.

Gabie, dimin. of *gab*, face.
Gabs, mouths.
Gage, went.
Gae, gave.
Gair, provident, saving.
Gait, road.
Gane, gone.
Gang, go.
Gar, make, cause.
Gars, makes.
Gash, chin, projecting under-jaw.
Gaun, going, gone.
Gear, wealth, property.
Ged, God (Cockneyfied Scots).
Get, beget.
Gey and, considerably, tolerably.
Ghaist, ghost.
Gie, give.
Gien, gi'en, given.

Gi'm, give him.
Gin, if.
Gin't, if it.
Girn, n. and f., snarl.
Glaiket, giddy, thoughtless.
Glammer, glamour.
Gled, kite, hawk.
Glegly, keenly.
Glunch, sour look.
Gouket sliep, stupid, coarse fellow.
Gouks, fools.
Gowany, daisied.
Gowd, gold.
Gowkit, foolish, stupid. *Gowkit fleeps* = *gouket sliep*[s].
Gowpens, handsful. A gowpen is the two hands held together to form a bowl.
Green, yearn for.
Greeting, crying, shedding tears.
Groat, old Scots coin, worth four-pence.
Gude losh ! Good Lord !
Guid, good.
Guiz, face countenance.
Gumshon, gumption, sense, quick-wittedness.
Gyte, mad.

Ha', hae, have.
Had, haud, hold.
Hads, holds.
Hae. See under *ha'*.
Hae and heil, wealth and health.
Hafflins, partially, scarcely.
Haggies, a haggis.
Hail, hale, whole.
Hain, save.
Hale. See under *hail*.
Hallan, partition-wall of a cottage
Hallanshaker, sturdy beggar, tramp.
Hally, holy.
Hameo'er, homely, rustic.
Hashes, blockheads.
Haud. See under *had*.
Haughs, rich low-lying lands.
Haund, hand.
Havers, idle, foolish talk.
Hawkie, a cow.

Hearty cock, jolly brisk fellow. A familiar term of address.
Hecht, promise.
Heft, dwelt, resided.
Herse, hoarse.
Hi', *hich*, high.
Hich. See under *hi'*.
Hizzie, a young woman.
Hoove, hoof.
Howm, holm, level ground at side of a stream.
Hudgemudge, secretly.
Hule. See under *Cust*.
Hun'er, hundred(s).
Hurlin', rushing, hurrying.
Hyne, away.

Ilk, each.
Ilka, every.
Ill-fawrd, unmannerly.
Ingle neuk, fire-side, chimney-corner.
Ingine, intellect, ability.
I'se, I shall.
Isna, is not.
Ither, other.

Jeel, congeal, grow cold.
Jeesies, wigs.
Jimply, scarcely.
Jinking, evasive.
Jouks, makes obeisance.

Kedgy, lively, wanton.
Kee, humour.
Keek, pry or look into.
Kelpies, water-sprites.
Ken, know.
Kend, *kent*, knew, known.
Kenna, know not.
Kent. See under *kend*.
Kintry, country.
Kirn, the last handful of grain cut down on the harvest field; harvest supper.
Kist, chest, trunk.
Knab, person of importance.
Know, knoll, hillock.
Kye, cows.
Kythe, show.
Laigh, low.

Laith, loath, unwilling.
Lallans, lowlands.
Lamie, dimin. of lamb.
Lat, let.
Lauchin, laughing.
Laucht, laughed.
Laun, land.
Lav'rock, lark.
Lawrit, Laureate.
Lear, learning, lore.
Leash o' lair, abundance of learning.
Lee, lie.
Len', lend, give.
Leuks, looks.
Lift, heaven, firmament.
Lightly'd, made light of.
Loe, love.
Loon, rascal (in a kindly sense).
Loot, let; *loot them be*, let them alone.
Louman, leg, limb.
Lout, bend low.
Lug, ear; pl., *lugs*.

Mair, *mare*, more.
Man, must.
Manna, must not.
Mare. See under *mair*.
Marled plaid, chequered plaid.
Marrow, equal.
Maud, shepherd's plaid.
Maun. See under *man*.
Mayna, may not.
Messin, cur, worthless dog.
Micht, might.
Midden, dunghill.
Mint, aim at, venture to.
Mirk, dark, black.
Misken, disown, ignore.
Mousie, dimin. of mouse.
Muckle, much.

Na, *nae*, not.
N'a'be, and all be.
Nae, no.
Neuk. See under *ingle*.
Niest, next.
Niffer, barter.
Nizz, nose.
Nouther, neither.

O', of.
O'erheeze, make one too vain.
Ony, any.
Orrow, odd, spare, unappropriated.
Ouk, owk, week.
Ousen, oxen.
Owk. See under *ouk*.
Owre, over ; too ; *owre sib to*, too much alike.

Parritch, porridge.
Pat, pot.
Pate, head.
Pattle, a plough staff.
Pervene, get the better of.
Pine, trouble, worry.
Pirn. See under *win' yer pirn*.
Pit, put.
Plack, copper coin of small value.
Plank, lay down.
Pleu, pleuch, pleugh, plough.
Pouch, pocket.
Pow, head.
Preachment timmer, matter for sermons.
Pree, pri', taste, sample.
Pried, tasted.
Priest-pushing, assailing the clergy.
Pruif, proof.
Pu', pull.
Pund, pound (weight).

Quean, woman.

Ragget cowt,
Rair, uproar.
Reekie's, Edinburgh's.
Reested, shrivelled.
Reez'd, praised.
Reezes, praises.
Refees'd, refused.
Rieft, plunder.
Rigg. See under *fur*.
Riving, tearing.
Roose, praise.
Rout, heavy blow.
Rout, commotion, disturbance.
Routs, pokes about.
Routh, abundance.

Rumming, foaming.
Rummle-gumption, common sense.

Sae, so.
Sair, sore.
Sair, greatly ; severe (study sair)·
Sair foot, time of need.
Sal, sall, shall.
Sang. " By my sang," *i.e.*, by my faith.
Sark, shirt.
Sa't, saut, salt.
Saul, soul.
Saut. See under *sa't*.
Saw, sow (grain).
Scour, drink off.
Scouth, freedom.
Scrieve, write.
Scrole, scroll.
Seil o' your face, " a phrase still used in Aberdeenshire expressive of a wish for happiness to, or a blessing on, the person to whom it is addressed." JAMIESON.
Shanks, legs.
Shaw, show.
Shool, shovel.
Shoon, shoes.
Sib, having like qualities.
Sic, such.
Siccan, such like.
Siller, money.
Simmer, Summer.
Sin', syn, since.
Sir Willie's notes, bank notes of the banking house of Sir William Forbes of Edinburgh.
Skair, share.
Skance, sight of, glance at.
Skelp, smack, slap.
Skelping whang, vigorous lash.
Skreed, write at length.
Skriech, screech.
Skunner, disgust.
Slee, slyly.
Sleekit, plausible, hypocritical.
Sleely-jibing, slyly jibing.
Sma', small.
Smeddam, mettle, spirit.

Smirkie, kissing.
Smoor'd, smothered.
Snib, cut short off.
Snull, a weakling, a craven.
Sonsy, sonsie, fortunate, happy.
Sou'd, sud, should.
Souf, hum.
Sough, sound, echo.
Soun', sound, make audible.
Soun', sound, whole.
Spaul, limb.
Speel, climb.
Speer, speir, ask for, inquire.
Spring, lively tune.
Spunk, spirit, pluck.
Spunkies, will-o'-the-wisps.
Sta', stall.
Staiggie, dimin. of *staig*, a stallion.
Stane, a weight of fourteen pounds.
Stang, sting.
Stappit, steeped.
Staun, stand.
Staunin', standing.
Steek, shut close.
Stirkie, dimin. of *stirk*, young ox.
Stirks, young oxen.
Stoited, stottit, staggered, stumbled.
Stout an' fell, strong and vigorous.
Strae, straw.
Straiks, strokes, blows.
Straught, straight.
Styme, particle (of time).
Sud. See under *sou'd*.
Sumphs, blockheads.
Sune, soon.
Sweir, unwilling.
Swelt, faint (from fright or nervousness).
Sybie, young onion.
Syn. See under *sin'*.
Syne, then.

Tacket, headless tacket, a headless nail.
Ta'en, taken.
Tak' tent, take care.
Tauntins, tauntings.

Teddy, ready for carting to the stock-yard.
Tent, give heed to.
Tether. See under *fankit*.
Teuch, tough.
Thackt, thatched.
Thestreen, yester-even.
Thoch, though.
Thol'd, suffered, endured.
Thole, suffer, endure.
Tholes, suffers.
Tho't, though it.
Thrang, crowd.
Ticht, neat, perfect.
Tift, good humour.
Till'd-up, turned up by the plough.
Till't, to it.
Tint, lost.
Toon, town.
Tosh, familiar, friendly.
Trow, believe.
Tulzie, broil, fight.
Tum, empty.
Twa, twae, two.
Twitch, touch.
Tykes, dogs.
Unco, uncommonly ; extraordinary.
Unco fain, uncommonly fond of ; extremely eager.

Vauntie, proud, vain.
Vitious, fierce.

Wa, wa', wall.
Wad, wager.
Wad, would.
Wadna, would not.
Wae, woe ; adj., sorrowful.
Waefu', woeful, sad.
Wae's, woe is.
Waesuck, alas !
Wal'd, chosen.
Wale, choice, selection, choicest.
Wall, well.
Wally, beautiful, pleasant.
Wallydraggle,
Walth, plenty, abundance.
Wanruly, unruly.
War, were.

Wark, work.
Warks, words.
Warran, warrant.
War't, were it.
Wat-mow'd, "wet mouthed," *i.e.*, fond of drinking.
Waur, worse.
Wean, child ; *weans*, pl.
Weel, well.
Weet, wet.
Weil-tauld, well told.
Wha, who.
Whang. See under *skelping.*
Whar, *whaur*, where.
Whase, whose.
Whiles, occasionally, sometimes.
Whilk, which.
Whin, furze.
Wi', *wie*, with.
Wightly, vigorously; *gh* guttural.
Win, dwell, reside.
Winna, will not.
Win't, winded.

Win' yer pirn, the meaning is, repent your conduct.
Winze, oath, curse.
Wirstle, wrestle.
Wissing, wishing.
Wittin, knowledge.
Wizen, gullet, windpipe.
Wonner, wonder.
Wordy, worthy.
Wrig, weakest of a brood of bird.
Wud, mad.
Wu'd, would.
Wyte, blame, fault.

Yad, *yade*, mare, horse.
Yavil, prostrate, helpless.
Ye'd, you would.
Yersel', yourself.
Ye'se, you shall.
Yill, ale.
Yird, earth.
Ye've, *y've*, you have.

GLOSSARY OF THE OBSOLETE ENGLISH WORDS IN TURNBULL'S POEM.

Aureat, golden.
Ay, always.
Besprent, bespread, besprinkled.
Dan, a word prefixed to names.
Eath, easy.
Eke, also.
Eftsoons, immediately.
Lig, to lie.
Moe, more.
Mote, might.
Mochel, much, great.
Ne, nor.
Passen, passing.
Soot, sweet, sweetly.

Unkempt, unadorned.
Ween, think, be of opinion.
Whilom, formerly.
Wight, a man.
Withouten, without, free from.
Yore, of old.
Yblent, blended, mingled.
Yclad, clad.
Yclep'd, called, named.
Ycover'd, covered.
Ymolten, melted, moved, soothed.
Ymove, to move.
Ypent, pent, shut up.

The letter Y is frequently placed at the beginning of a word by Spenser to lengthen it a syllable.